To Swapna and Sanjana

STOCHASTIC MODELS
OF DECISION MAKING
IN ARRANGED MARRIAGES

Amitrajeet A. Batabyal

University Press of America,® Inc.

Lanham · Boulder · New York · Toronto · Oxford

CONTENTS

LIST OF TABLES

FOREWORD

Anyone who is even cursorily familiar with the institution of marriage knows that outside North America and Western Europe, arranged marriages are commonplace. Further, what is interesting to note is that even in a country like the United States, high divorce rates, combined with increasing numbers of "dating services" and "introduction agencies" suggest both dissatisfaction with the *status quo* and interest in this heretofore strange kind of marriage.

Although there is a Gary Becker-inspired literature on the economics of marriage, as best as I can tell, this literature pays virtually no attention to arranged marriages. Further, it also seems to me that the formal modeling of arranged marriages is still in its infancy. Given this regrettable state of affairs, it is indeed a pleasure to commend Professor Batabyal's new book on decision making in arranged marriages. Certainly, Professor Batabyal does not analyze all aspects of the complex world of arranged marriages. However, what his book does do very well is to break new ground on a much neglected research area. In particular, Professor Batabyal's book ably shows how formal modeling, and particularly stochastic modeling, can shed light on various aspects of decision making in arranged marriages.

This book marks the culmination of original and high quality research conducted in the past decade by Professor Batabyal, and the book itself is an important contribution to the social science literature in general and to the economics literature in particular. As such, it should be of great interest to all theoretically inclined researchers in the social sciences.

Logan, Utah   Basudeb Biswas
August 2005

PREFACE

The impetus for conducting scholarly research on the subject of decision making in arranged marriages arose out of an animated conversation with a friend some years ago about the pros and cons of arranged versus love marriages. As I delved into the social sciences literature in general and the economics literature in particular to learn more about what other scholars have said about decision making in arranged marriages, I realized that from a theoretical perspective, very little had been said and that this subject was hence largely virgin territory for research.

Armed with this knowledge, I began to construct and analyze theoretical models of decision making in arranged marriages. This led to a series of papers in academic economics journals in the last decade and this book represents my attempt to synthesize this body of research on the subject of decision making in arranged marriages. Given the nature of the subject, my approach in this book is explicitly probabilistic. I show how the theory of stochastic processes and the techniques of stochastic modeling can be used to shed valuable light on the nature of decision making in arranged marriages. It is my hope that this book will encourage economists—and social scientists more generally—to conduct both theoretical and empirical research on a subject of considerable importance in contemporary times.

Rochester, New York   Amitrajeet A. Batabyal
September 2005

ACKNOWLEDGMENTS

Of the ten essays in this book, nine have appeared previously in different journals. Therefore, I would like to take this opportunity to express my appreciation to various publishers for granting me permission to reprint these previously published essays. "Spouse Selection in Arranged Marriages: An Analysis of Time Variant and Time Invariant Decision Rules" originally appeared in the *Journal of Economic Research* in Vol 8, pp 187-201, 2003, and I thank the Hanyang Economic Research Institute and the editors of the journal for their help. "Aspects of Arranged Marriages and the Theory of Markov Decision Processes" originally appeared in *Theory and Decision* in Vol 45, pp 241-253, 1998, and I thank Springer Science and Business Media for their kind permission to reprint this paper. "On Decision Making in Arranged Marriages with a Stochastic Reservation Quality Level" and "On the Likelihood of Finding the Right Partner in an Arranged Marriage" originally appeared in *Applied Mathematics Letters* in Vol 16, pp 933-937, 2003, and in the *Journal of Socio-Economics* in Vol 30, pp 273-280, 2001, respectively, and I thank Elsevier for permission to reprint these two papers. "A Dynamic and Stochastic Analysis of Decision Making in Arranged Marriages," "Meetings and Exposure Before an Arranged Marriage: A Probabilistic Analysis," and "Arranged or Love Marriage? That is the Question" all originally appeared in *Applied Economics Letters* in Vol 6, pp 439-442, 1999, in Vol 11, pp 473-476, 2004, and in Vol 9, pp 893-897, 2002, respectively, and I thank Taylor and Francis <http://www.tandf.co.uk> for their assistance. Finally, I note that "On Strategy and the Likelihood of Success in Marital Matchmaking Under Uncertainty" and "A Game Model of Dowry Determination in an Arranged Marriage Context" both appeared previously in *Economics Bulletin*, in Vol 10, pp 1-7, 2004, and in Vol 10, pp 1-8, 2005, respectively.

This book would not have seen the light of day without the assistance of two sets of individuals. The first set consists of Hamid Beladi, and I thank him for allowing me to include our co-authored work in this book. The second set consists of Cass Shellman (at RIT) and Ruby Vázquez (at USU), and I thank these ladies for all manner of assistance with this book. In addition, I thank the Gosnell endowment at RIT for the requisite financial support.

My wife Swapna and my daughter Sanjana both make sacrifices, and, as a result, I am able to pursue my intellectual interests as best as I see fit. As such, I thank them both for their love and their support. It means a lot to me.

Amitrajeet A. Batabyal
Rochester, NY
September 2005

CHAPTER 1—
INTRODUCTION TO STOCHASTIC MODELS OF DECISION MAKING IN ARRANGED MARRIAGES

ABSTRACT

This book has one central objective and that is to demonstrate how the theory of stochastic processes and the techniques of stochastic modeling can be used to effectively model arranged marriage settings, and to use these stochastic models of arranged marriages to explain various aspects of the nature of decision making in arranged marriages. To this end, this chapter first provides a succinct introduction to arranged marriages and then it delineates the contributions of each of the book's nine analytical chapters.

Key words: arranged marriage, decision making, stochastic modeling, theory

1. PRELIMINARIES

In western "love" marriages, men and women who wish to get married seek out their partners themselves. In other words, individuals looking to get married search (presumably optimally) for a groom or a bride and this search activity is conducted primarily, if not exclusively, by the two individuals who are interested in getting married. In contrast, in eastern "arranged" marriages, the parties who wish to get married do not conduct any search activities by themselves. Instead, the process of searching for an apposite bride or groom is conducted by parents, other family members, and increasingly, matchmaking intermediaries. It is common in many modern arranged marriages for the well-wishers of a marrying individual to bring what they believe are suitable marriage prospects to this individual for his or her approval. If a particular prospect is approved, then, broadly speaking, the search process terminates. If, on the other hand, the prospect under consideration is not approved, then the search process continues. Within this general schema, many variations are possible. For instance, groom and bride seekers generally have *asymmetric* bargaining power. As a result, *ceteris paribus*, women will tend to have less say than men in the ultimate selection of a marriage partner.[1]

Arranged marriages were the norm rather than the exception in many countries until the 19th century but today, in this era of globalization, this form of marriage is less popular than it once was. Even so, arranged marriages are still widely practiced in the Indian subcontinent (India, Pakistan, Bangladesh, Sri Lanka, and Nepal) and it is fair to say that it is the dominant form of marriage in this part of the world. In addition to this part of the world, arranged marriages are also common in parts of Africa, the Middle East, and East Asia. Consistent with an earlier observation, even though arranged marriages were very popular in large parts of China, Japan, and South Korea, in contemporary times, western style "love" marriages have made considerable inroads in these East Asian nations.

Proponents of arranged marriages have claimed that such marriages are more successful than love marriages. A perspective that is often offered in this regard by supporters is that in an arranged marriage, as opposed to a love marriage, a man and a woman begin a relationship on *neutral* territory, with no expectations from each other. Over time, as the relationship matures, a significant sense of understanding develops between the two individuals. Why should this be the case? The typical arguments that are offered by proponents are that this is likely because the very logic of an arranged marriage dictates that the two involved parties come from similar social, economic, and cultural backgrounds. In addition, or so goes the argument, while the primary basis for consummating a love marriage is physical attraction, in an arranged marriage, this aspect, while not irrelevant, is certainly de-emphasized by the pertinent well-wishers of the two involved individuals. These then are some of the reasons why arranged marriages are, it is claimed, likely to work. If the metric of divorce rates is used to measure the extent to which marriages work then it is certainly true that the divorce rate in countries in which marriages are mostly "love," is higher than countries in which marriages are mostly "arranged."

There is now a substantial literature—largely descriptive and case study based—on the pros and cons of arranged and love marriages. Therefore, the basic goal of this book is *not* to contribute to this literature.[2] Instead, given the near absence of formal modeling in the extant literature in economics on arranged marriages and the scant attention that has been paid by this literature to decision making processes, the central objective of this book is to show how stochastic models can be used to better understand various aspects of the nature of decision making in arranged marriages. Because the subject of decision making in an arranged marriage context is fundamentally all about decision making under *uncertainty*, by using probabilistic models we hope to shed valuable light on this subject.

Now, given that the basic search activities in an arranged marriage are being conducted by a marrying agent's well-wishers and not by him or her directly, one key question that arises in this context is this: When should an agent or individual wishing to have an arranged marriage say yes to a marriage proposal and not wait any longer? Chapter 2 uses the theory of Markov decision processes to shed light on this salient question and it is to this probabilistic analysis that we now turn.

2. THE INDIVIDUAL ESSAYS

2.1. *Arranged Marriages and Markov Decision Processes*

Many problems in economics require us to optimally and sequentially control one or more stochastic processes. What often happens in such problems is that a decision maker observes the state of a stochastic process at distinct points in time. After each observation, this decision maker takes an action. The sequence of actions taken by the decision maker interacts with the random conditions to influence the evolution of the underlying stochastic process. As noted by Derman (1970) and Ross (1974), the mathematical abstraction of this kind of problem is referred to as either a Markov decision process (MDP) or as discrete dynamic programming.

Now recall that the key question to be answered in Chapter 2 is the following: When should an agent wishing to have an arranged marriage say yes to a marriage proposal and not wait any longer? The theory of MDPs can be used to answer this question. To proceed further, the marrying agent under study must decide on a policy, i.e., a rule for choosing actions. Chapter 2 uses a particular stationary policy, namely, the one stage look ahead policy (OSLAP). With this policy, our marrying agent compares the option of stopping immediately (saying yes now to a marriage proposal) with the option of waiting for an additional step and then stopping (saying yes later). If the stopping region determined by the OSLAP is a closed set, i.e., if this region is an absorbing set for the state variable, then the use of the OSLAP is optimal.

The analysis conducted in Chapter 2 leads to a number of findings. First, the stopping set, under the OSLAP, is characterized mathematically. Second, given the optimal stopping framework of this chapter, a question that needs to be resolved concerns the status of formerly rejected proposals. In other words, is it possible for our marrying agent to recall a previously rejected marriage proposal. Moreover, does the answer to the "when to say yes" question depend on whether or not previously rejected proposals can be recalled. Theorem 1 tells us that in the theoretical framework of this chapter, the answer to the "when to say yes" question is *invariant* to the recall of previous marriage proposals.

Before we comment on the implications of theorem 1, the reader should understand some of the intricacies in the analysis that is undertaken in this chapter. In this regard, it should be noted that once the assumptions that are required for the modeling have been made, the ensuing analysis suggests that the marrying agent's optimal policy has an intuitive form: accept the proposal whose utility is at least some threshold level. However, it is important to realize that this seemingly intuitive policy is *not* optimal because the stopping region defined by this policy is not an absorbing set for the state variable. Therefore, it is necessary to modify the intuitive rule so that the stopping region is, in fact, a closed set. Once this has been done, the use of the OSLAP is optimal and hence theorem 1 follows.

Chapter 2's theorem 1 tells us that the answer to the "when to say yes" question is *invariant* to the recall of previous marriage proposals. Put differently, this theorem says that under the OSLAP, the optimal "yea saying" rule depends *only* on the properties of the current marriage proposal, independent of whether there is recall of previous proposals. This means that the transience of a marriage proposal has no bearing on the answer to the "When to say yes" question. From a practical standpoint, the implication of this finding is that an agent wishing to get married in an arranged marriage setting need not make his or her marriage decision more conservative simply because proposals, if not acted upon immediately, will be lost.

The analysis in Chapter 2 unquestioningly assumes that the marrying agent under study has already made a decision to get married. Therefore, the pertinent issue in this chapter involves ascertaining *when* this agent should say yes to a specific marriage proposal. However, in general, it is certainly possible that a marrying agent operating in an optimal stopping framework of the sort described in this chapter *may* not get married at all. Therefore, it is certainly interesting to explore the nature of the marriage decision when this possibility is accounted for. This exploration is carried out in Chapter 3.

2.2. Decision Making in Arranged Marriages

In the Chapter 3 model, it is assumed that while family and friends look for acceptable marriage prospects, it is the marrying agent under study who finally decides when to say yes to a marriage proposal. This agent receives proposals as a result of the search activities undertaken by others. His or her decision is to determine which proposal to say yes to. Upon receipt, a specific marriage proposal is either accepted or rejected and, obviously, part of a proposal cannot be accepted or rejected. This means that the marriage decision is *indivisible*. Further, it is assumed here that this marriage decision is *irreversible* as well.[3] Finally, in this Chapter 3 model, the nature of the marriage decision is explored in a model in which the agent may not get married at all. This eventuality arises because the marrying agent's objective is to maximize the *likelihood* of accepting the best possible marriage proposal, when these proposals are received sequentially over time.

The theory of optimal stopping—see Harris (1987) and Dixit and Pindyck (1994)—is used to comprehend the nature of the marrying agent's choice problem. This agent receives statistically independent marriage proposals that are of uncertain quality, sequentially, in discrete time. The analysis in this chapter initially focuses on the case of a known finite number—say n—of marriage proposals. As in Chapter 2, upon receipt of a proposal, our marrying agent must decide whether to accept the proposal (say yes to marriage) or reject the proposal (say no to marriage) and wait for additional proposals. Upon receipt of a proposal, the marrying agent is able to rank this proposal in terms of its quality. Hence, the only information that this agent is privy to is the relative rank of a proposal, as compared to former proposals. The marrying agent's aim is to maximize the *probability* of accepting the best (highest quality) marriage proposal when all $n!$ orderings of the various proposals are equally likely.

The analysis in Chapter 3 shows that our marrying agent's optimal policy (OP) has the following structure: For some marriage proposal $l \leq n\text{-}1$, reject the first l proposals, i.e., say no to marriage, and then accept (say yes to) the first so-called "candidate" marriage proposal. Having determined the OP, the natural next task is to compute the likelihood of accepting the marriage proposal of the highest quality when the above OP is used. The answer to this question is provided by this chapter's theorem 1. Specifically, this theorem tells us that our marrying agent ought to reject the first $(1/e)$ fraction of marriage proposals and then (s)he should accept the first candidate proposal thereafter.

Theorem 1 tells us that when faced with the prospect of receiving a large number of proposals sequentially, our marrying agent should initially say no to marriage, i.e., (s)he should reject the first $(1/e)$ fraction of all proposals. (S)he should then say yes to the first candidate proposal. The chance that the use of this OP will result in the best proposal being accepted is $(1/e) = 0.37$. This last finding has an important implication: Irrespective of how actively friends, family, and intermediaries look for marriage proposals, if our marrying agent insists on saying yes only to the highest quality proposal, (s)he may *never* get married.

To intuitively see why an OP of the type described in theorem 1 makes sense, observe that there is an asymmetry associated with the marrying agent's yes/no decision. From the perspective of this agent, a no decision always leads to future options, but a yes decision terminates the probabilistic proposal generation process. Hence, there is a *premium* associated with a no decision because this decision preserves flexibility. The policy described in theorem 1 optimally trades off this flexibility premium with the likelihood that the highest quality proposal will be lost if the agent waits too long to say yes.[4]

The theoretical analysis in Chapter 3 shows that, *inter alia*, it may be optimal for the marrying agent to never say yes to a proposal, i.e., to never get married. The reader should understand that this result has nothing to do with the marrying agent's time or decision making horizon. Instead, it arises because the marrying agent's optimization problem involves the maximization of a probability. What happens when a marrying agent uses the following decision rule: Get married as long as the quality of a marriage proposal exceeds a *stochastic* reservation quality level? This hitherto unstudied question is analyzed in Chapter 4.

2.3. *A Stochastic Reservation Quality Level*

Looked at along the temporal dimension, the decision problem faced by our marrying agent in Chapter 4 concerns when (if ever) to say yes to a marriage proposal. Alternately, looked at along the marriage proposal dimension, this agent's decision problem concerns which proposal (if any) to say yes to. The marrying agent in this chapter solves his or her decision problem in a dynamic and stochastic framework. Further, as in Chapter 3, this chapter also supposes that the marriage decision is both indivisible and irreversible.

Now, upon receipt of a proposal, our marrying agent must decide whether to say yes to the proposal (get married) or to reject the proposal (stay unmarried) and wait for additional proposals. As in Chapter 2, to continue the analysis, it is necessary to specify a decision rule for our marrying agent. To this end, Chapter 4 analyzes the properties of the following simple decision rule: Let M_0, M_1, M_2, M_3, . . . be random variables that denote the quality of the marriage proposals that are received sequentially over time. Put differently, M_0 is the quality of the first marriage proposal, M_1 is the quality of the second marriage proposal, and so on and so forth. In this chapter, it is assumed that the marrying agent's *random* reservation utility level is M_0, the quality of the first marriage proposal. Given this utility level, our marrying agent's decision rule is to accept the first proposal that exceeds M_0 in quality.

Next, Chapter 4 defines N to be a positive and integer valued random variable—that can also be interpreted as an index for the first proposal whose quality level exceeds the reservation quality level M_0—and then it computes the probability mass function for N. This computation yields four interesting attributes of the arranged marriage decision. First, for any finite N, the probability of saying yes to a marriage proposal (getting married) is always positive. Second, the maximal likelihood of getting married is ½ and this probability occurs when $N=1$. Third, as N rises, the probability of getting married falls over time. Finally, in the limit as $N \to \infty$, the likelihood of getting married is zero. Together, these four attributes tell us that the likelihood of getting married is higher early in the marrying agent's time and decision making horizon. Citing the work of Blood (1967) and Mullatti (1992), Chapter 4 points out that this last finding is indeed consistent with reality.

Given that the probability of getting married is positive for all finite N, it is interesting to determine the average wait before the marrying agent under study is able to say yes to a proposal. Specifically, given the limiting result of the previous paragraph, is it possible that in a mean waiting time sense our marrying agent will never get married? To answer these questions, Chapter 4 computes the expected value of N and then demonstrates that even though the probability of getting married for all finite N is positive, the mean wait until marriage is *infinity*. Thus, the analysis here shows that in an average waiting time sense, our marrying agent will *never* say yes to a marriage proposal (always stay unmarried).

The above result complements a finding in Chapter 3. Specifically, the previous paragraph's last result tells us that even when a marrying agent's focus is *not* on maximizing the odds of accepting the best marriage proposal, the use of the decision rule described in this chapter along with the *stochastic* reservation quality level can still slant—in a mean waiting time sense—a marrying agent's decision in the direction of no arranged marriage. Further, the analysis here shows that for an agent who really wishes to have an arranged marriage, the use of this chapter's decision rule is undesirable because in expected value terms, a marrying agent following this rule will end up single.

In the Chapters 2 and 3 analyses of decision making in arranged marriages, the marrying agent's decision problem is modeled in a way that precludes considerations of age at marriage. In both of these chapters, the agent does not care *when* in his or her lifetime (s)he gets married. This is at odds with known facts about arranged marriages (see Blood (1967) and Mullatti (1992)). In addition, Chapters 2-4 have not studied the properties of *time variant* decision rules which are not only more realistic but which also permit a marrying agent to be flexible over the length of his or her decision making horizon. Finally, Chapters 2-4 also have not conducted a *comparative* analysis of the relative merits of time invariant and time variant decision rules. These salient issues are addressed in Chapter 5.

2.4. Time Invariant and Time Variant
Decision Rules

To stress the age dimension of the arranged marriage decision, the analysis in Chapter 5 supposes that the agent under study wishes to be married by time T. It also assumes that if the agent fails to get married by time T, then his or her utility is zero. The reader will recognize that there is an asymmetry associated with the binary choice accept/reject decision. If the marrying agent under study rejects a particular proposal then (s)he can always accept a later proposal as long as (s)he accepts this proposal by time T. In contrast, if our agent accepts a particular proposal ((s)he gets married), then his or her well-wishers will not bring any more proposals to him or her. In other words, a decision to reject a proposal preserves future options whereas a decision to accept a proposal does not. This asymmetry and the age constraint together play a basic role in the analysis presented in Chapter 5.

Now, in order to accomplish his or her goal of getting married by time T, the marrying agent will need to use a decision rule. Two decision rules, the first time *invariant* and the second time *variant*, are analyzed in this chapter. When using the time invariant rule, our agent first selects a threshold level of utility $\hat{U}$ that is *independent* of time. Then, (s)he accepts the first proposal whose utility exceeds $\hat{U}$. For the time variant decision rule, the threshold level of utility is itself a function of time t. Therefore, instead of working with a fixed $\hat{U}$, our agent now works with a *time dependent* threshold $\hat{U}(t)$, where $\hat{U}(t) = (1-t)/(3-t)$.

Given the above specification of the two distinct decision rules, the next task in this chapter is to first compute and then compare our marrying agent's expected utility which each of these two decision rules. The computation of our marrying agent's expected utility with the time invariant decision rule involves setting up and then solving a specific expected utility maximization problem. The analysis in this part of Chapter 5 shows that if our marrying agent chooses $\hat{U}^* = 0.2079$, then (s)he will have maximized his or her expected utility. Because this chapter uses specific functional forms, it is also possible to conclude that the optimized value of the agent's expected utility is 0.330425 with the time invariant decision rule. Can the marrying agent under study do better by using a time variant decision rule? This question is addressed next in Chapter 5.

With the time variant decision rule, for obvious reasons, an optimal utility threshold $\hat{U}^*$ cannot be computed. Even so, it is still possible to ascertain the maximized value of our agent's expected utility when (s)he uses this decision rule.

After several computational steps with specific functional forms, this chapter shows that the highest level of expected utility that our agent can hope to attain with the time variant decision rule $\hat{U}(t) = (1-t)/(3-t)$ is 0.333333. On the basis of this result, Chapter 5 conducts a comparative analysis of the two kinds of decision rules and this comparative exercise yields three conclusions.

First, in the time invariant case, the optimal value of the utility threshold $\hat{U}$ is fixed and this value does *not* change with the passage of time. In contrast, when our marrying agent's decision rule is time variant, the utility threshold is *always* a function of time and hence its optimal value changes over time. Second, relative to a time invariant decision rule, a time variant decision rule permits a marrying agent to be flexible and hence adaptable in the face of changing circumstances. Finally, the second point notwithstanding, the premium associated with the maintenance of temporal flexibility—and hence adaptability—in decision making is positive but not large. As is noted in Chapter 5, this last result is most likely due to the fact that a relatively simple time variant decision rule has been used to conduct the underlying analysis.

Given the salience of the age issue in arranged marriages, like Chapter 5, Chapter 6 also analyzes this issue, albeit from a different perspective. In particular, a key question that is not addressed explicitly in chapter 5 is the likelihood that the use of a particular decision making process will result in our marrying agent finding the *right* partner for himself or herself. In its analysis of the age issue, chapter 6 also addresses this rightness issue.

2.5. *Finding the Right Partner*

As in Chapter 5, the focus here is on an agent who wishes to be married by a particular age, say T years of age. This agent has a utility function defined over marriage proposals that has a deterministic part and an additive stochastic part. The deterministic part is known to the marrying agent *and* to his or her well-wishers. The additive stochastic part is known *only* to the marrying agent. This modeling strategy is intended to capture the view that well-wishers generally have a good but not perfect idea about the agent's preferences regarding his or her choice of marriage partner.

When a proposal is brought to the marrying agent, this agent can either say yes to the proposal or reject it and wait for additional proposals. If a particular proposal is rejected by the agent, then his or her well-wishers will bring a subsequent proposal to the agent only if they believe that this proposal is of higher quality. Further, our marrying agent knows that his or her well-wishers will act in this manner. Consequently, in a stochastic sense, the marrying agent's objective is to say yes to the *last* proposal that is received before time T.

Now given the results of Chapter 3, suppose that in order to accomplish this objective, our marrying agent decides to wait a while, and then say yes to the first proposal that is brought to him or her. Is this a desirable strategy when there is an explicit age constraint? How long should the agent wait before saying yes? Finally, if our agent uses this strategy, what is the likelihood that (s)he will accomplish his or her objective? These are the outstanding questions that remain to be answered.

Suppose our agent decides to wait for w units of time, before saying yes to a marriage proposal that is brought to him or her. Obviously, $w\varepsilon[0,T]$. The task now is to determine the optimal length of our marrying agent's waiting period. To do this, Chapter 6 first computes the likelihood that only a single proposal is brought to the agent under study in the time interval $[w,T]$. This likelihood function is then used to set up and solve a particular optimization problem. The solution to this optimization problem is the optimal length, w^*, that is sought.

A comparative statics exercise yields two interesting results about the optimal wait period w^*. First, it is shown that, *ceteris paribus*, an increase in the age by which our agent would like to be married has the effect of lengthening the period of time for which it is optimal to wait before saying yes to a marriage proposal. Second, all else being equal, if the rate at which the agent's well-wishers receive marriage proposals increases, then, too, it is optimal for this agent to wait longer before accepting a marriage proposal.

The analysis in Chapter 6 complements both the analysis in Chapter 3 and the "value of waiting to invest" result from the investment under uncertainty literature.[5] In particular, this analysis demonstrates that the optimal course of action for an agent who wishes to have an arranged marriage by the time (s)he is T years of age, involves waiting a while, and then saying yes to the proposal that is brought to him or her. We are now in a position to discuss the most interesting question that is addressed in this chapter: What is the likelihood of finding the *best* partner? The analysis here shows that this probability is $(1/e) \approx 0.37$. This tells us that the cooperation of well-wishers, coupled with the pursuit of an optimal strategy will enable our marrying agent to do quite well in finding the right partner in an arranged marriage.

As Blood (1967), Rao and Rao (1982), Applbaum (1995) and others have pointed out, in contemporary arranged marriage settings, the individual wishing to marry has considerable autonomy over the actual marriage decision and, on occasion, it is even possible for this individual to veto a specific marriage proposal. This ability to veto arises because it is now common for the marrying individual's facilitators to set up one or more meetings with prospective partners. As a result of these meetings, prospective partners get *exposed* to our marrying individual. Now, this exposure level is a *random* variable. In addition, this random variable clearly has a nontrivial bearing on the ultimate likelihood of marriage.[6] Even so, to the best of our knowledge, the extant literature on arranged marriages in economics has paid no attention whatsoever to this exposure level random variable. Given this state of affairs, the purpose of Chapter 7 is to shed light on the stochastic properties of this exposure level random variable.

2.6. Meetings and Exposure Before an Arranged Marriage

If our marrying agent expresses interest in a particular proposal that is brought to him or her, then his or her facilitators will generally arrange one or more meetings with the person behind the proposal. As a result of these meetings, two things happen. First, a potential partner gets exposed to our marrying agent. Second, our marrying agent forms an opinion about a potential partner and, therefore, the meetings may increase or decrease the ultimate likelihood of marriage with this particular person.

Three questions are of particular interest in Chapter 7. In this regard, note that our marrying agent's facilitators are interested in the exposure level random variable z because the likelihood of marriage is a function of z. In other words, these facilitators are interested in the stochastic properties of z conditional on a marriage being consummated. This is the first of this chapter's three questions.

In contrast, the interests of the people acting on behalf of potential partners are a little different. Clearly, these people are also interested in the first question that we have just stated. However, because arranged marriages are common in more traditional societies in which excessive pre-marital male/female mixing is frowned upon, these people are risk averse and hence they will not want to diminish a partner's future marriageability by getting him or her too exposed—by way of meetings—to an agent with whom ultimate marriage is improbable.[7] From a modeling perspective, the effect of all this is that people acting on behalf of the potential partners are also interested in the stochastic properties of the exposure level random variable z but conditional on a marriage *not* being consummated. This is the second of Chapter 7's three questions.

The outstanding task now is to compute the conditional probability density function of the exposure level random variable z, first conditioned on a marriage taking place and then conditioned on a marriage not taking place. Mathematically, the objective is to calculate $g(z/marriage)$ and $g(z/no\ marriage)$. This is because the answer to the first (second) question is given by $g(z/marriage)$ $(g(z/no\ marriage))$. After computing expressions for these two density functions, Chapter 7 asks: What is the *optimal* level of exposure for potential partners? This chapter comments on the practical relevance of this question and then it shows that the previously calculated expressions for the two density functions are useful precisely because they can be used by our marrying agent's facilitators and by the people acting on behalf of potential partners to set up the objective function part of a suitably formulated optimization problem. The solution to such a problem will give us the answer to the question posed a few sentences back.

The third and final question that is analyzed in Chapter 7 is the following: Is there a monotonicity relationship between the probability $Prob(z)$[8] and the ratio $g(z/marriage)/g(z/no\ marriage)$? In other words, is it the case that if $Prob(z)$ is increasing (decreasing) in z then the above ratio is also increasing (decreasing) in z? The answer to this question is provided in two parts. First, it is shown that the above ratio can, for all practical purposes, be expressed as the ratio of the probability of getting married to the probability of staying single. Next, calculus is used to verify that a monotonicity relationship *does* exist between the probability *Prob*(z) and the ratio $g(z/marriage)/g(z/no\ marriage)$, which is also the *relative* conditional probability density function of the exposure level random variable z. The answer to this third question tells us that, in a sense, the study of the trinity of meetings, exposure levels, and an arranged marriage can be reduced to a study of the above specified monotonicity relationship.

The analyses in Chapters 2 through 7 have, for the most part, focused on the properties of specific decision making rules in the context of arranged marriages. The last three chapters of this book depart from this line of research and provide additional—and quite different—perspectives on decision making in arranged marriages. Specifically, Chapter 8 takes up and sheds theoretical light on a popular question in the comparative literature on marriage and that question is this: Is an agent contemplating marriage better off with an arranged marriage or with a love marriage?

2.7. *Arranged or Love Marriage?*

Agents considering marriage today face a clear choice. They can either go the arranged marriage route or they can go the love marriage route. Specific aspects of western style love marriages have been studied by Hu (2001), Nakosteen and Zimmer (2001), and Fraser (2001). Similarly, alternate facets of arranged marriages have been analyzed by Martin and Tsuya (1991), Feng and Quanhe (1996), and by Chapters 2 through 7. These studies have undoubtedly advanced our understanding of various aspects of arranged and love marriages. Even so, because there are *no* comparative theoretical analyses of the desirability of arranged versus love marriages, we still know very little about whether an agent is better off with an arranged or a love marriage. Given this state of affairs, Chapter 8 conducts a comparative theoretical analysis of the pros and cons of arranged versus love marriages.

Suppose that our marrying agent chooses the love marriage route. In this case, (s)he meets potential partners in accordance with a Poisson process with rate β.[9] If our agent decides to date a particular partner, then it takes this agent L units of time to decide whether (s)he would like to marry this particular partner. If the agent decides that (s)he would like to marry the partner in question, then (s)he proposes to the partner, this partner accepts, and the two individuals are married right away. Our marrying agent may decide, for instance, that (s)he is better off with an arranged marriage. In this case, the agent's well-wishers take upon themselves the task of finding this agent a partner. The agent's well-wishers take a random amount of time to find an apposite partner and the expectation of this time is A.

In Chapter 8, the agent under study uses the following straightforward decision rule: Once the decision to get married has been made, our agent gives himself or herself w units of time to be successful with the love marriage option. If (s)he fails to find someone suitable by himself or herself within w time units, then (s)he gives the arranged marriage option a chance. Note that the default option in this scenario is love marriage. Next, Chapter 8 computes the mean time to marriage, $E[marriage\ time]$, when our agent adopts the above decision rule. With this computation in place, it is now possible to answer the comparative question that is explicit in the title of this chapter.

Given that our agent has already decided that (s)he would like to get married, it makes sense for him or her to minimize the mean time to marriage. In this connection, the analysis in Chapter 8 shows that $d\{E[marriage\ time]\}/dw = \exp(-\beta w)\{1+\beta(L-A)\}$. By inspection, when $\{(1/\beta)+L\} > A$, the previous derivative is positive and hence the mean time to marriage is minimized by setting $w=0$. Further, it is shown here that $\{(1/\beta)+L\}$ is the expected total time it takes our agent to get married if (s)he chooses the love marriage option. On the other hand, A is the average time it takes our agent's well-wishers to find him or her a partner. Hence, the inequality $\{(1/\beta)+L\} > A$ tells us that if the mean total time taken to get married via the love marriage option exceeds the average time it takes to get married via the arranged marriage option, then our agent should forswear the love marriage option (set $w = 0$) and instead choose the arranged marriage option.

In contrast, when $\{(1/\beta)+L\} < A$, the mean total time to marriage via the love marriage option is less than the average total time it takes to get married via the arranged marriage option. Accordingly, in this case, our agent should relinquish the arranged marriage option (set $w=\infty$) and instead go with the love marriage option. Finally, in the knife-edge case in which $\{(1/\beta)+L\}=A$, all values of w give the same mean time to marriage and hence our agent is indifferent between the arranged and the love marriage options.

At various points in this introductory chapter we have alluded to the increasingly salient role played by matchmakers in pairing agents who wish to get married via the arranged marriage route. In addition, although matchmakers have traditionally been used in the Orient, they are now becoming popular in the Occident as well.[10] Given this state of affairs, a number of hitherto unstudied and yet interesting questions about the activities of these matchmakers emerge. Chapter 9 provides a stochastic analysis of three such questions.

2.8. Marital Matchmaking Under Uncertainty

Matchmakers attempt to pair male and female agents with similar aspirations, goals, and interests. In addition, all matchmakers conduct their business in inherently *probabilistic* environments. The three questions concerning the activities of matchmakers that are addressed in Chapter 9 are the following: First, what are the properties of alternate matchmaking strategies? Second, given a specific matching strategy, what is the mean number of successes that a matchmaker can hope for? Finally, given a desired number of successes, is it possible to make a mathematically precise statement about the likelihood that the number of matching successes will be at least the desired number? As is pointed out in Chapter 9, these questions deserve attention not only because they are of considerable practical relevance but also because economists have paid virtually no attention to them.

To answer the previous paragraph's first question, Chapter 9 initially stipulates two desirable strategies—the "local" strategy and the "global" strategy—for matching male and female agents.[11] Specifically, there are n male and n female agents and our matchmaker's job is to match each male agent to one and only one female agent. Every time the matchmaker assigns a male agent to a female agent, (s)he incurs a cost and $c(j,k)$ is the cost incurred by our matchmaker when (s)he matches male agent j to female agent k, j, $k=1, \ldots, n$.

The first or "local" matching strategy works as follows: The matchmaker begins by assigning male agent 1 to the female agent who results in the lowest cost to him or her, the matchmaker. In other words, male agent 1 is matched with female agent k_1, where $c(1,k_1) = \min_{(k)} c(1,k)$. Then, the matchmaker assigns male agent 2 to female agent k_2 so that $c(2,k_2) = \min_{\{k \neq k_1\}} c(2,k)$. The matchmaker continues in this manner until all male and female agents have been matched. This local strategy is useful because it always selects the best female match for the male agent currently under consideration.

The second desirable strategy is a "global" version of the previous paragraph's local strategy. Using this global strategy, the matchmaker first considers all n^2 cost values and (s)he selects the pair $(j_1 k_1)$ for which his or her cost $c(j,k)$ is minimal. The matchmaker then matches male agent j_1 to female agent k_1. Next, (s)he discards from further consideration all cost values that involve either male agent j_1 or female agent k_1. Hence, $(n-1)^2$ cost values now remain and our matchmaker continues the process of selecting pairs and then matching as just described. This global strategy is desirable because it is a more thorough version of the local strategy.

Next, Chapter 9 ascertains the expected total cost incurred by our matchmaker when (s)he uses the local and the global strategies. The detailed analysis in this chapter leads to theorem 1 and this theorem contains the interesting but counterintuitive result that the expected total cost to our matchmaker is the *same* for both strategies. The obvious implication of this theorem is that it does not matter which strategy our matchmaker uses because both strategies lead to the same total expected cost. This chapter next addresses the remaining two questions that we stated in the first paragraph of this section.

In this regard, it is first noted that a match is a success if it leads to marriage within T time periods. Then, using the theory of Bernoulli random variables,[12] it is shown that the average number of successes is given by the product of the number of matches (n) and the success probability of each match (p). We now address the question about the probability that the number of matching successes is at least some desired number. In response to this third question, chapter 9 provides a tight upper bound on the probability that the number of matching successes is at least $1+\theta$ times the mean number, where θ is any positive number. The analysis of this third question tells us that if we use the mean number of successes np as our benchmark, then there *is* a tradeoff between a higher desired number of matching successes and the probability that these desired successes will in fact materialize.

Now, shifting the focus away from matchmaking, there is no gainsaying the fact that, even today, dowries are a part of many arranged marriages. Even though the literature on dowries is sizeable, there are important questions about dowries that deserve additional research attention from social scientists in general and economists in particular. One such question is the following: Given that mediators are frequently used to determine the actual amount of a dowry payment, what is the nature of the interaction between this mediator and the bride and the groom's families? A game theoretic model is used in Chapter 10 to analyze this salient question.

2.9. Dowry Determination in an Arranged Marriage

In a country like India, in contemporary times, the practice of dowry has changed substantially from what it used to be in antiquity. In a disproportionate number of arranged marriages in India and elsewhere, dowry payments are anything but voluntary. The actual amount of the dowry that is demanded in any specific instance is closely connected to the economic and to the social status of the groom's family. In this regard, Sheel (1999, p. 18) tells us that the higher the socioeconomic status of the groom's family, the higher is generally the demand for dowry. Further, the work of Jaggi (2001) and Reddy (2002) tells us that in many arranged marriage settings, the bride and the groom's families conduct dowry negotiations with the help of a *mediator*. This state of affairs raises an important question: What is the nature of the interaction between a mediator and the two concerned families?

To answer this question, Chapter 10 casts the mediator in the role of an arbitrator and then this chapter analyzes a game model of dowry determination. There are three players. A representative from the bride's family referred to as the *bride b*, a representative from the groom's family referred to as the *groom g* and the mediator designated with the letter *m*. The timing of the game between these three players is as follows: First, the bride and the groom simultaneously make dowry offers d_b and d_g, respectively. Second, the mediator selects one of these two offers as the final dowry amount that is agreed upon by both the bride and the groom. Chapter 10 supposes that the mediator has a preferred dowry amount in mind denoted by d_m. Further, it is also supposed that after observing the offers d_b and d_g, the mediator simply picks the offer that is closer to his preferred amount d_m.

Mathematically, we expect $d_g > d_b$ and the analysis in Chapter 10 shows that this inequality does indeed hold in equilibrium. Given this state of affairs, the mediator's choice problem can be described as follows. He selects d_b if $d_m < (d_b + d_g)/2$ and he selects d_g if $d_m > (d_b + d_g)/2$. The mediator obviously knows d_m but from the perspective of both the bride and the groom, d_m is a *random* variable. Therefore, the next task in this chapter is to compute the probabilities that d_b and d_g are selected by our mediator. Once this has been done, we can mathematically express the mediator's expected dowry amount as d_b *Prob* {d_b *is selected*} + d_g *Prob* {d_g *is selected*). Now, in general, the bride (groom) will want the dowry to be as low (high) as possible. Therefore, the strategy adopted in Chapter 10 is to suppose that the bride wants to *minimize* the mediator's expected dowry amount and that the groom wants to *maximize* this same amount.

This gives rise to two optimization problems and the solution to these two optimization problems yields two specific results. First, we see that in equilibrium, the *mean* of the two dowry offers from the bride and the groom equals the *median* of the mediator's preferred dowry amount. Second, we learn that the gap between the two dowry offers made by the groom and the bride must equal the reciprocal of the value of the density function at the median of the mediator's preferred dowry amount. Now, to shed additional light on the dowry determination problem, Chapter 10 considers two cases. In the first (second) case the mediator's preferred dowry amount d_m is normally (beta) distributed. This discussion with specific functional forms is revealing in at least two ways. To see this, consider the d_m is normally distributed case. In this case, Chapter 10 shows that the equilibrium dowry offers made by the bride and the groom are centered around the mean of the mediator's preferred dowry amount. Second, we also learn that the difference between these two offers is essentially a function of the bride and the groom's *uncertainty* about the mediator's preferred dowry amount. Specifically, as this uncertainty increases (decreases), the difference between the two equilibrium dowry offers also increases (decreases).

3. CONCLUSIONS

Arranged marriages in general and decision making in arranged marriages in particular are both fascinating subjects that have, unfortunately, received scant attention thus far in the economics literature. Given this unsavory state of affairs, our objective in this book is to demonstrate how the theory of stochastic processes and the techniques of stochastic modeling can be used to effectively model arranged marriage settings, and to use these stochastic models of arranged marriages to explain various aspects of the nature of decision making in arranged marriages. To this end, in this introductory chapter, we have highlighted the ways in which the analyses in the individual chapters collectively help accomplish this book's stated objective. The theoretical modeling of arranged marriages and decision making in arranged marriages are still very much in their infancy. Therefore, in the coming years, one may look forward to many interesting developments in theoretical research in these broad and interesting subjects.

REFERENCES

Alvarez, L. "Arranged Marriages get a Little Rearranging." *New York Times*, 22 June 2003.
Applbaum, K.D. "Marriage with the Proper Stranger: Arranged Marriage in Metropolitan Japan." *Ethnology* 34 (1995): 37-51.
Auboyer, J. *Daily Life in Ancient India*. New York, NY: Macmillan Press, 1965.

Berger, J. "Family Ties and the Entanglements of Caste; Pressure to Live by an Outmoded Tradition is Still Felt Among Indian Immigrants." *New York Times*, 24 October 2004.

Derman, C. *Finite State Markovian Decision Processes*. New York: Academic Press, 1970.

Blood, R.O. *Love Match and Arranged Marriage: A Tokyo-Detroit Comparison*. New York: Free Press, 1967.

Dixit, A.K., and R.S. Pindyck. *Investment Under Uncertainty*. Princeton, N.J.: Princeton University Press, 1994.

Fathi, N. "Tehran Journal; Marriages Made Not in Heaven but in a Cleric's Office." *New York Times*, 11 November 2003.

Feng, W., and Y. Quanhe. "Age at Marriage and the First Birth Interval: The Emerging Change in Sexual Behavior Among Young Couples in China." *Population and Development Review* 22 (1996): 299-320.

Fraser, C.D. "Income Risk, the Tax-Benefit System, and the Demand for Children." *Economica* 68 (2001): 105-25.

Gautham, S. "Coming Next: The Monsoon Divorce." *New Statesman*, 18 February 2002.

Goode, W.J. *World Revolution and Family Patterns*. New York: Free Press, 1963.

Harris, M. *Dynamic Economic Analysis*. New York: Oxford University Press, 1987.

Hu, W. "Welfare and Family Stability: Do Benefits Affect When Children Leave the Nest?" *Journal of Human Resources* 36 (2001): 274-303.

Jaggi, T. "The Economics of Dowry: Causes and Effects of an Indian Tradition." *University Avenue Undergraduate Journal of Economics* 4 (2001): 1-19. http://www.econ.ilstu.edu/UAUJE.

Mace, D., and V. Mace. *Marriage: East and West*, Garden City, N.Y: Doubleday and Company, 1960.

Mandelbaum, D.G. *Society in India*. Berkeley: University of California Press, 1970.

Martin, L.G., and N.O. Tsuya. "Interactions of Middle-Aged Japanese With Their Parents." *Population Studies* 45 (1991): 299-311.

McDonald, R., and D. Siegel. "The Value of Waiting to Invest." *Quarterly Journal of Economics* 101 (1986): 707-28.

Moore, M. "Changing India, Wedded to Tradition: Arranged Marriages Persist With 90s Twists." *Washington Post*, 8 October 1994.

Mullatti, L. "Changing Profile of the Indian Family." In *The Changing Family in Asia*, edited by Y Atal. Bangkok, Thailand: UNESCO, 1992.

Nakosteen, R.A., and M.A. Zimmer. "Spouse Selection and Earnings: Evidence of Marital Sorting." *Economic Inquiry* 39 (2001): 201-13.

Pindyck, R.S. "Irreversibility, Uncertainty, and Investment." *Journal of Economic Literature* 29 (1991): 1110-52.

Rao, V.V.P, and V.N. Rao. *Marriage, the Family and Women in India*. New Delhi, India: South Asia Books, 1982.

Reddy, S. "Ancient Practice of Dowry Perpetuates Violence Against Women in India." *Digital Freedom Network* (2002). http://www.asiaobserver.com/ India-story2.htm.

Ross, S.M. "Dynamic Programming and Gambling Models." *Advances in Applied Probability* 6 (1974): 593-606.

Ross, S.M. *Stochastic Processes*, 2nd ed. San Diego, Cal.: Academic Press. 1996.

Ross, S.M. *Introduction to Probability Models*, 7th ed. San Diego, Cal.: Harcourt Academic Press, 2000.

Ross, S.M. *Probability Models for Computer Science*. San Diego, Cal.: Harcourt Academic Press, 2002.

Sheel, R. *The Political Economy of Dowry*. New Delhi, India: Manohar Publishers, 1999.

Winston, W. *Operations Research Applications and Algorithms*. Cambridge, Mass.: Duxbury Press, 1997.

NOTES

1. For more on these and related matters, see Alvarez (2003), Fathi (2003), and Berger (2004).

2. For more on this literature, see Mace and Mace (1960), Goode (1963), Auboyer (1965), Mandelbaum (1970), Moore (1994), Gautham (2002), and Berger (2004).

3. The intent here is to capture the fact that in most societies in which arranged marriages are prevalent, once an agent agrees to a marriage proposal, it is generally difficult for him or her to renege on the original decision, at least in the short run.

4. This result is related to the "value of waiting" result in the investment under uncertainty literature. For more on this, see McDonald and Siegel (1986), Pindyck (1991), and Dixit and Pindyck (1994).

5. For more on this literature, the reader should consult Pindyck (1991) and Dixit and Pindyck (1994).

6. For more on this topic, go to http://www.askasia.org/frclasrm/readings/r000153.htm and to http://www.youthinformation.com/infopage.asp?snID=805.

7. The reader should understand that because of asymmetries in the bargaining power of men versus that of women, in most arranged marriage settings, these considerations are more relevant for female partners. This also means that the significance of the second question—that we state at the end of this paragraph—declines if the marrying agent under study is a woman.

8. Recall that the exposure level of a potential partner to our marrying agent is denoted by z. An exposed potential partner will ultimately get wedded to our marrying agent with some probability and this probability is denoted by $Prob(z)$.

9. For more on the Poisson process, see Ross (1996, pp. 59-97).

10. For an interesting account of matchmaking activities in an arranged marriage context in Iran, see Fathi (2003).

11. These strategies are variants of the so-called "greedy algorithms." For more on these algorithms and related issues, such as the assignment problem, see Winston (1997) and Ross (2000, 2002)

12. See Ross (2000, pp. 27-28; 2002, pp. 6-7) for more on Bernoulli random variables.

CHAPTER 2—
ASPECTS OF ARRANGED MARRIAGES
AND THE THEORY OF MARKOV
DECISION PROCESSES

ABSTRACT

The theory of Markov decision processes (MDP) can be used to analyze a wide variety of stopping time problems in economics. In this chapter, the nature of such problems is discussed and then the underlying theory is applied to the question of arranged marriages. We construct a stylized model of arranged marriages and, *inter alia*, it is shown that a decision maker's optimal policy depends only on the nature of the current marriage proposal, independent of whether there is recall (storage) of previous marriage proposals.

Key words: Markov decision process, arranged marriage, decision making

1. INTRODUCTION

Many problems in the social sciences involve the optimal sequential control of certain kinds of stochastic processes. In such problems, a stochastic process is observed at various points in time to be in one of a number of possible states. After each observation, a decision maker takes one of many possible actions. The sequence of actions taken by the decision maker interacts with the probabilistic environment to affect the evolution of the underlying stochastic process. The mathematical abstraction of this kind of problem is called a Markov decision process (MDP).[1] While the theory of MDPs has been widely used to study problems in the operations research literature, this theory has been applied considerably less frequently in economics. This holds true despite the fact that economic problems as varied as land development over time and under uncertainty, biodiversity conservation in a dynamic and stochastic framework, and the timing of marriage in an arranged marriage context, are all amenable to analysis with the theory of MDPs.

The arranged marriage problem is of particular interest. Not only have arranged marriages been around for several centuries, they are the rule rather than the exception in many parts of Africa, Asia, and the Middle East.[2] Despite this phenomenon, economists have paid scant attention to arranged marriages. Indeed, the economics literature on the subject of marriage—pioneered by Becker (1973, 1991)—has largely restricted itself to an analysis of marriage in a deterministic setting, in the context of Western societies. As such, there exists very little formal knowledge about the nature of decision making in arranged marriages.

Given this state of affairs, this chapter has two objectives. First, we shall demonstrate the scope of MDPs by analyzing arranged marriages specifically, and by discussing other problems such as land development and biodiversity conservation. Second, by focusing on the question "When should an agent wishing to have an arranged marriage say yes to a marriage proposal and not wait any longer," we shall demonstrate the surprising implications of certain decision making rules and thereby increase our understanding of decision making in arranged marriages.

The rest of this chapter is organized as follows. Section 2 provides a theoretical description of MDPs and a stylized model of decision making in arranged marriages. Section 3 discusses our understanding of arranged marriages in the context of the section 2 findings. Section 4 provides a discussion of our understanding of decision making which emerges from the findings of section 2. Finally, section 5 concludes and offers suggestions for future research.

2. MDPs AND ARRANGED MARRIAGES

Becker (1991, p. 324) has noted that imperfect information is a key feature of decision making in the marriage market. This observation applies with equal force in the context of arranged marriages as well. The logic of arranged marriages tells us that because of a variety of reasons such as (i) imperfect and incomplete information stemming from limited social experiences and travel opportunities (Goode 1963, p. 210), and (ii) the tendency of young people to seek pleasure (Auboyer 1965, p. 176), young persons generally cannot be trusted to find a suitable mate for themselves. As a result, parents, relatives, and increasingly matchmaking intermediaries, take upon themselves the task of looking for a suitable bride (or groom). While in western countries, the agent wishing to marry generally looks for a mate himself (or herself), in an arranged marriage, this important task is not undertaken by the agent but by his (or her) family, friends, and intermediaries. This is a fundamental difference between arranged marriages and marriages in western countries.

The second relevant aspect of arranged marriages concerns the marrying agent's decision. As Rao and Rao (1982, pp. 32-33) have noted, in contemporary arranged marriage settings, the agent wishing to marry has considerable autonomy over the actual marriage decision. That is, while family and friends look for suitable marriage prospects, it is the agent who decides when to say yes. This agent receives marriage proposals as a result of the investigative activities undertaken by others. His (or her) decision is to decide which proposal to say yes to. Clearly, this marriage decision is indivisible; for the purpose of this chapter we shall assume that it is irreversible as well.[3] Formally, the agent's decision problem is one of optimal stopping.[4]

The theory of MDPs can be used to understand the nature of the marrying agent's choice problem. To this end, let us begin with a general framework of decision making.[5] Consider a stochastic environment in which our agent who seeks to be married receives marriage proposals sequentially in discrete time. The environment is stochastic because the decision to get married depends on the receipt of marriage proposals; these are of uncertain quality. It is assumed that successive marriage proposals are statistically independent, and that the distribution from which these proposals are drawn is fixed and known to the marrying agent (decision maker). Let $X(t)$ be the proposal that is received at time t. If we denote the quality of this proposal by j, then mathematically, we have $Prob(X(t) = j) = P_j$. As discussed earlier, this receipt of proposals is the result of investigative activities undertaken by the marrying agent's family, friends, and intermediaries. The cost of this investigative activity results in disutility to the agent; in what follows, we assume that the agent altruistically incorporates this disutility in his (or her) overall decision problem.[6]

On receiving a marriage proposal, the agent decides whether to say yes to this proposal, or to delay marriage and wait for additional proposals. This decision is based on the agent's utility from saying yes. Let $H(\cdot)$ be the continuous and strictly monotone function that maps proposals to utility. In other words, if $X(t)$ is the marriage proposal received at time t, then $U(t) = H(X(t))$ denotes the utility from saying yes, given that a decision to say yes has been made. Note that because $H(\cdot)$ is a continuous and strictly monotone transformation of $X(t)$, for all t, it follows that the successive utilities $\{U(t): t > 0\}$ are also statistically independent, and drawn from a distribution that is fixed and known to the marrying agent (for details, see Wolff 1989).

The decision to say no to a specific proposal results in utility as well as disutility to our agent. The nature of the marriage decision is such that there is an asymmetry associated with the yes/no decision. A "no" decision always leads to future options, but a "yes" decision terminates the stochastic proposal generation process.[7] As such, the utility from saying no stems from the fact that the agent preserves the flexibility to receive new proposals—of possibly higher quality—in the future.[8] The disutility arises from the fact that the investigative activities of friends, relatives, and intermediaries resulting in the receipt of proposals are costly. We shall denote the net utility from saying no, i.e., the net utility of preserving flexibility, by B.

In order to choose an action, our marrying agent must decide on a policy, i.e., a rule for choosing actions. Policies can be of varying levels of complexity. For instance, a specific policy may depend on the history of marriage proposals; alternately, it may be randomized in the sense that it chooses an action with a certain probability. An important subset of the set of all policies is the set of stationary policies. A policy is said to be stationary if it is nonrandomized, and if the action it chooses at time t depends only on the state of the process (marriage proposals) at time t. Stationary policies serve as useful "rules of thumb," also, the behavioral implications of such policies can be determined in a relatively straightforward manner. Consequently, in this chapter we shall restrict our attention to stationary policies. Rather than provide an exhaustive analysis of every kind of stationary policy, we shall illustrate the nature of such policies by focusing on the one stage look ahead policy (OSLAP). When using this policy, a decision maker (for instance, our marrying agent) compares the option of stopping immediately (saying yes now) with the option of waiting for an additional step and then stopping (saying yes later). If the stopping region determined by the OSLAP is a closed set, i.e., if this region is an absorbing set for the state variable, then the use of the OSLAP is optimal.

Let the state at any time t be denoted by the 2-tuple $\{t, U(t)\}$, where $U(t)$ is the utility that will be received, should the agent choose to say yes at time t. The reader should note that with this specification of the state, we have a two action—say yes or say no—MDP. This is because the OSLAP is a stationary policy and because the sequence of states $\{U(t): t = 0,1,2...\}$ forms a discrete time Markov chain. Now suppose that our marrying agent is able to recall previous marriage offers. In other words, this agent is able to say yes to a proposal that he (or she) had previously said no to. In this connection, the two extreme cases are that of perfect recall and no recall. In the former case every previously turned down proposal may be recalled at some later date. In the latter case, it is not possible to recall any proposal that has been declined previously. In what follows, we shall analyze the implications of recall on the marrying agent's decision as to when he (or she) should say yes to a specific marriage proposal.

With perfect recall, the state at any time t will be the maximum utility that can be obtained from saying yes to a proposal at that time. Now the transition probabilities at any time t for the countable state Markov chain $\{U(t): t, 0\}$ are given by [9]

$$P_{ij}(t) = 0 \; if \, i > j, \tag{2.1}$$

$$P_{ij}(t) = \sum_{r=0}^{r=i} P_r, if \; i = j, \tag{2.2}$$

and

$$P_{ij}(t) = P_j, \; if \; i < j. \tag{2.3}$$

Equation (2.1) tells us that under the OSLAP, the utility Markov chain will not go to state j if the utility in state j is less than the utility in state i. Hence, $P_{ij}(t) = 0$. Equation (2.2) tells us that if the utilities in states i and j are equal, then under the OSLAP the probability of making a transition from state i to state j is the sum of all the probabilities of receiving utility of amount 0 through i. Finally, equation (2.3) tells us that if the utility in state j exceeds the utility in state i, then under the OSLAP the Markov chain will move to state j with transition probability P_j.

We shall now characterize the stopping region defined by the OSLAP. This region corresponds to the set of states for which saying yes in state i is at least as good as saying no and waiting for exactly one more time period and then saying yes. This stopping region is given by

$$S = \left\{ i : i \geq \sum_{r=0}^{r=i} iP_r + \sum_{j=i+1}^{\infty} jP_j + B \right\}. \tag{2.4}$$

The first term on the RHS of the weak inequality in equation (2.4) is obtained from equation (2.2); this term denotes the expected utility in states 0 through i. The second term is obtained from equation (2.3); this term denotes the expected utility in states $i + 1$ through infinity. Finally, the third term is the net utility from saying no and waiting. After some algebra, equation (2.4) can be further simplified to

$$S = \{i : 0 \geq E[\max (U - i, 0)] + B\}. \tag{2.5}$$

In equation (2.5), $E[\cdot]$ denotes the expectation operator, $\max(\cdot)$ denotes the maximum operator, and U denotes utility. The reader will note that because $\max(U - i, 0)$ decreases in i, the maximum utility from saying yes (agreeing to marry) cannot decrease with time. This means that the stopping region described by S is an absorbing set for the state variable $U(t)$. Now, assuming stability of the utility Markov chain,[10] the OSLAP involves saying yes at the first instance in which the utility from saying yes is at least i^*, where i^* solves

$$i^* = \min \{i : 0 \geq E[\max (U - i, 0)] + B\}. \tag{2.6}$$

It is important to note that under the OSLAP, the optimal policy *never* recalls a previously declined proposal. This means that recall—whether perfect or partial—is irrelevant to the question of deciding when to say yes to an arranged marriage proposal. We have just demonstrated

Theorem 1: *In the theoretical framework of this chapter, the answer to the "when to say yes" question is invariant to the recall of previous marriage proposals.*

Theorem 1 tells us that under the OSLAP, the optimal "saying yes" rule depends only on the nature of the current marriage proposal, independent of whether there is recall of previous proposals. Alternately put, the transience of a marriage proposal has no bearing on the answer to the "When to say yes" question. From a practical standpoint, this means that an agent wishing to get married in an arranged marriage setting need not make his marriage decision more conservative simply because proposals, if not acted upon immediately, will be lost. We now discuss, in turn, some of the implications of this analysis for our understanding of arranged marriages in particular and sequential decision making in general.

3. DISCUSSION: OUR UNDERSTANDING OF ARRANGED MARRIAGES

Consider the question of the robustness of Theorem 1. In this connection let us note that the only two assumptions that we needed to obtain the result described in this theorem are (i) that the successive marriage proposals be statistically independent, and (ii) that the distribution from which these proposals are generated be fixed and known to the marrying agent (decision maker). Both these assumptions are fairly standard and they are not overly restrictive. However, consider the case in which these assumptions do not hold. If the offers are statistically dependent, then it would not be possible to characterize the state by the 2-tuple $[t, U(t)]$. Alternately put, in the Markov decision theoretic framework of this chapter, we could not represent the state by the marrying agent's utility. Further, it would not be optimal to stop the utility stochastic process by using a decision rule such as the OSLAP. If the distribution function from which the proposals are drawn is not known to the marrying agent, then the problem becomes substantially more complicated. In particular, we would now have a dynamic problem with an element of inference as well as decision. In this situation, one can construct scenarios in which the marrying agent first goes through a period of learning and then he (or she) makes a decision.

The model analyzed in this chapter is a partial equilibrium model. In other words, we have studied the marriage decision from the perspective of one agent; as such, this analysis is unable to say much about a market equilibrium. However, it should be noted that this chapter is not intended to be an analysis of an arranged marriage market equilibrium. The basic objective here is to show that (i) an important real world phenomenon can be effectively modeled using the theoretical construct of MDPs, and that (ii) once this modeling exercise has been carried out, a rather surprising result—described in Theorem 1—obtains.

From an institutional perspective, i.e., arranged marriages in most Asian countries, recall (storability) is really more of an issue for males who tend to have greater bargaining power. In this connection, the reader should note that the fact that agents on the other side of the marriage market are also possibly making decisions sequentially does not make recall a logical impossibility. It seems reasonable to think of scenarios where agents on both sides of the market are able to say yes to a previously declined offer. Having said this, it is perhaps most important to note that in the final analysis, recall does not matter and the optimal stopping (when to say yes) rule depends only on the nature of the current marriage offer, independent of whether there is recall of previous offers.

It has already been shown that introducing a net benefit term (B) to saying no, and allowing for the possibility of recall does not make the use of the OSLAP and the associated stopping set described by the OSLAP suboptimal. Introducing additional wrinkles such as discounting or the non-inclusion of the disutility stemming from the investigative costs borne by family and friends in the marrying agent's decision problem would not change anything either; the essence of Theorem 1 would continue to hold. So we conclude this section by noting that while other characterizations of arranged marriages are possible, we do believe that our analysis offers one interesting and robust characterization.

4. DISCUSSION: OUR UNDERSTANDING OF DECISION MAKING

The collection of assumptions that are contained in this chapter represents the minimum number of assumptions that are necessary to tractably model the underlying arranged marriage problem. In particular, the modeling framework of this chapter is interesting and worth knowing more about because it has wide applicability in economics.[11]

The reader will note that once the two assumptions that are required for the analysis have been made, the first task is to recognize that the marrying agent's optimal policy appears to have an intuitive form: accept the proposal whose utility is at least some threshold level. The next task involves recognizing that the use of this kind of an intuitive policy will not be optimal because the stopping region defined by this policy is not an absorbing set for the state variable. As a result, one then has to modify the intuitive rule so that the stopping region is a closed set. Once this has been done, the use of the OSLAP is optimal and hence Theorem 1 follows. Moreover, the assumptions and the use of the OSLAP are necessary and sufficient for the result described in this theorem. This tells us that the seemingly obvious decision rule that one would want to use is actually suboptimal; in fact some work is required to determine the exact nature of the marrying agent's optimal policy.

To shed more light on our understanding of sequential decision making, it helps to consider the class of stopping problems which have the property described in Theorem 1. This class of problems has the following attributes: (i) successive realizations of the state variable are independent and drawn from a fixed and known distribution, (ii) stopping is an option in all states, (iii) the problem is stable, (iv) the stopping region is closed, and (v) the horizon is unity. In problems with these attributes, recall is typically not an issue. However, in problems where recall is an issue, whether or not there is declining marginal benefit to recall depends on what can and cannot be recalled and the cost of such recall. When recall costs are zero and all proposals can be recalled, there is no declining marginal benefit to recall. However with convex recall costs and with limited ability to recall past proposals, a declining marginal benefit phenomenon will typically be present.[12]

Let us conclude this section by noting that in models where recall does matter, the use of a stationary policy such as the OSLAP will generally be suboptimal. Second, the decision maker's problem will now look more like a search and stop problem in which the object that is being sought can move between the various cells in which the search is being conducted, and the decision maker has the option of revisiting a previously searched cell. The combination of these two features suggests that more general stopping rules—such as the n stage look ahead policy— should be used to determine when the decision maker should stop in these "recall matters" cases.

5. CONCLUSIONS AND EXTENSIONS

In this chapter we used the theory of MDPs to formally study the question of marriage in an arranged marriage setting. In particular, an answer to the "When to say yes" question was provided. This answer involved a probabilistic comparison of the utility from saying yes at time t, i.e., $U(t)$, with the expected utility from saying no (delaying marriage) and waiting for new proposals beyond time t. Our analysis shows that a marrying agent's optimal stopping rule depends only on the nature of the current marriage proposal, independent of whether there is recall of previous proposals. One can extend the analysis of this chapter by studying arranged marriage situations in which the marrying agent's role is not definitive but only consultative. This will involve analyzing a different kind of stopping problem. In particular, this kind of study will permit richer analyses of the connections between the investigative activities of family and friends and this modified "When to say yes" question. Second, one can also analyze the impact of non-stationary policies on the marrying agent's decision problem. Such an analysis will enable us to have a better understanding of the connections between alternate forms of decision making and the decision to get married.

As discussed in the previous sections, the theoretical framework of this chapter is interesting and worth knowing more about because it has wide applicability in economics. Indeed, problems as diverse as land development and biodiversity conservation over time and under uncertainty can be effectively modeled using this theoretical framework. To see how, consider the land development problem. A developer has the option of developing his land at any one of several points in time. This decision to develop will depend on a probabilistic comparison of the profit from developing now with the profit from waiting now and developing later. This is a stopping time problem and it can be analyzed in a Markov decision theoretic framework. Indeed, this kind of analysis will nicely complement existing work on this question by Arrow and Fisher (1974), Henry (1974), Capozza and Helsley (1990), and Clarke and Reed (1990).

As regards the conservation of biodiversity, consider Swanson's (1995) perspective on this matter. Swanson (1995) has argued that the global decline in biodiversity is best viewed as a process of conversion in which naturally existing species have been systematically replaced by human selected ones. If one views this habitat conversion process as a stochastic process, then the theory of MDPs can be used to model a regulator's problem as a stopping time problem in which the central regulatory task is to halt this conversion process at an appropriately determined point in time. An analysis of this problem along these lines will usefully extend extant work by Swanson (1995) and others on the biodiversity conservation question. In these and other ways, the theory of MDPs can be used to shed light on a number of important and currently outstanding problems in economics.

REFERENCES

Arrow, K.J., and A.C. Fisher. "Environmental Preservation, Uncertainty, and Irreversibility." *Quarterly Journal of Economics* 88 (1974): 312-319.

Auboyer, J. *Daily Life in Ancient India.* New York: Macmillan Press, 1965.

Batabyal, A.A. "The Impact of Information on Land Development: A Dynamic and Stochastic Analysis." *Journal of Environmental Management* 50 (1997): 187-192.

Becker, G.S. "A Theory of Marriage: Part I." *Journal of Political Economy* 81 (1973): 813-846.

———. *A Treatise on the Family*, enlarged edition. Cambridge: Harvard University Press, 1991.

Capozza, D.R., and R.W. Helsley. "The Stochastic City." *Journal of Urban Economics* 28 (1990): 187-203.

Clarke, H.R., and W.J. Reed. "Land Development and Wilderness Conservation Policies Under Uncertainty: A Synthesis." *Natural Resource Modeling* 4 (1990): 11-37.

Derman, C. *Finite State Markovian Decision Processes*. New York: Academic Press, 1970.

Dixit, A.K., and R.S. Pindyck. *Investment Under Uncertainty*. Princeton, N.J.: Princeton University Press, 1994.

Goode, W.J. *World Revolution and Family Patterns*. New York: Free Press, 1963.

Henry, C. "Option Values in the Economics of Irreplaceable Assets." *Review of Economic Studies* 41 (1974): 89-104.

Mandelbaum, D.G. *Society in India*. Berkeley: University of California Press, 1970.

McDonald, R., and D. Siegel. "The Value of Waiting to Invest." *Quarterly Journal of Economics* 101 (1986): 707-728.

Moore, M. "Changing India, Wedded to Tradition: Arranged Marriages Persist With 90s Twists." *Washington Post*, 8 October 1994.

Otani, K. "Distributions in the Process to Marriage and Pregnancy in Japan." *Population Studies* 45 (1991): 473-487.

Pindyck, R.S. "Irreversibility, Uncertainty, and Investment." *Journal of Economic Literature* 29 (1991): 1110-1152.

Rao, V.V.P., and V.N. Rao. *Marriage, the Family and Women in India*. New Delhi, India: South Asia Books, 1982.

Ross, S.M. *Applied Probability Models with Optimization Applications*. San Francisco, Cal.: Holden-Day, 1970.

———. "Dynamic Programming and Gambling Models." *Advances in Applied Probability* 6 (1974): 593-606.

———. *Introduction to Stochastic Dynamic Programming*. San Diego, Cal.: Academic Press, 1983.

Stone, L.D. *Theory of Optimal Search*. New York: Academic Press, 1975.

Swanson, T.M. "The International Regulation of Biodiversity Decline: Optimal Policy and Evolutionary Product." In *Biodiversity Loss*, edited by C. Perrings, K.G. Maler, C. Folke, C.S. Holling, and B.O. Jansson. Cambridge: Cambridge University Press, 1995.

Wolff, R.W. *Stochastic Modeling and the Theory of Queues*. Englewood Cliffs, N.J.: Prentice Hall, 1989.

NOTES

1. Some researchers—such as Derman (1970) and Ross (1974)—have used the term "discrete dynamic programming" to describe similar problems.
2. For a more detailed corroboration of this claim, see Mandelbaum (1970), Moore (1994), Otani (1991), and Rao and Rao (1982).
3. By making this assumption, we wish to capture the fact that in most societies in which arranged marriages are prevalent, social pressures are such that once the agent agrees to a marriage proposal, it is generally difficult for him (or her) to renege on the original decision, at least in the short run. We do not wish to imply that separation and/or divorce is never an option for the agent.
4. It should be noted that while the marrying agent's role described here is increasingly the prevalent one, it is not the only possible role. In some arranged marriage settings, the agent's role is largely consultative. For more on this, see section 5.
5. This framework is based on Batabyal (1997).
6. The case in which the agent acts selfishly and does not incorporate this disutility is a special case of this more general formulation. This is discussed at the end of section 3.
7. Also see footnote 3.
8. This is related to the "value of waiting" result in the investment under uncertainty literature. For more on this, see McDonald and Siegel (1986), Pindyck (1991), and Dixit and Pindyck (1994).
9. Note that the i, j correspond to utility levels in state i and j, respectively.
10. See Ross (1970, p. 135) for a necessary and sufficient stability condition.
11. This is explained in greater detail in the following section.
12. Readers may be wondering about the relationship between our model and a search model. To this end, we note that while there is no direct relationship between our model and a general search problem, search problems which have a stopping option to them are related to the model of this chapter. In particular, if one is prepared to make a number of assumptions, then one can convert this latter class of "search and stop" problems into an optimal stopping time problem of the sort analyzed in this chapter. For more on this, see Stone (1975).

CHAPTER 3—
A DYNAMIC AND STOCHASTIC ANALYSIS
OF DECISION MAKING IN ARRANGED
MARRIAGES

ABSTRACT

In a recent paper, Batabyal (1998) has analyzed the decision making process in arranged marriages. In particular, Batabyal shows that a marrying agent's optimal policy depends only on the nature of the current marriage proposal, independent of whether there is recall of previous marriage proposals. In this chapter, this line of enquiry is continued by focusing on the decision problem faced by a marrying agent who wishes to maximize the probability of getting married to the best possible person. *Inter alia*, it is shown that this agent's optimal policy calls for waiting a while, and saying yes to the first candidate thereafter.

Key words: arranged marriage, decision making, probability, recall

1. INTRODUCTION

"Marriage is popular," said George Bernard Shaw, "because it combines the maximum of temptation with the maximum of opportunity." This popularity notwithstanding, economists have been interested in systematically studying marriage only since Becker (1973). Further, this interest has largely been restricted to the study of marriage in a deterministic setting, in the context of western societies (Becker, 1991). In non-western societies, arranged marriages have been around for several centuries. Indeed, they are the rule rather than the exception in large parts of Africa, Asia, and the Middle East.[1] Despite this phenomenon, economists in general have paid scant attention to arranged marriages. Consequently, very little is known about the nature of decision making in such marriages.

Given this state of affairs, this chapter has two objectives. First, we shall formulate and analyze a model of decision making in arranged marriages. In particular, we shall focus on the following question: When should an agent wishing to have an arranged marriage say yes to a marriage proposal and not wait any longer? Second, we shall discuss some of the implications of our findings for our understanding of arranged marriages.

The rest of this paper is arranged as follows: Section 2 provides an overview of arranged marriages and a brief review of the relevant literature. Section 3 provides a detailed description and an analysis of a stylized model of decision making in arranged marriages. Finally, section 4 concludes and offers suggestions for future research.

2. ARRANGED MARRIAGES: AN OVERVIEW

Becker (1991, p. 324) has noted that imperfect information is a key feature of decision making in the marriage market. This observation applies with equal force in the context of arranged marriages as well. The logic of arranged marriages tells us that because of a variety of reasons such as (i) imperfect and incomplete information stemming from limited social experiences and travel opportunities (Goode, 1963, p. 210), and (ii) the tendency of young people to seek pleasure (Auboyer, 1965, p. 176), young persons generally cannot be trusted to find a suitable partner for themselves. Consequently, parents, relatives, and increasingly matchmaking intermediaries, take upon themselves the task of looking for a suitable bride (or groom). While in western countries, the agent wishing to marry generally looks for a partner himself (or herself), in an arranged marriage this important task is not undertaken by the agent but by his (or her) family, friends, and intermediaries.[2] The reader should note that this is a fundamental difference between arranged marriages and marriages in western nations.

The second germane aspect of arranged marriages concerns the marrying agent's decision. As Rao and Rao (1982, pp. 32-33) have noted, in contemporary arranged marriage settings, the agent wishing to marry has considerable autonomy over the actual marriage decision. In other words, while family and friends look for appropriate marriage prospects, it is the agent who decides when to say yes. This agent receives marriage proposals as a result of the investigative activities undertaken by others. His (or her) decision is to decide which proposal to say yes to. Clearly, this marriage decision is indivisible. For the purpose of this chapter, we shall assume that it is irreversible as well.[3]

Recently, Batabyal (1998) has analyzed a model of decision making in arranged marriages. Batabyal shows that a marrying agent's optimal policy depends only on the nature of the current marriage proposal, independent of whether there is recall of previous marriage proposals. Batabyal's approach implicitly assumes that the marrying agent has already made a decision to get married; as such, the relevant issue in this paper involves determining when the agent should say yes to a specific marriage proposal. In this paper, we shall explore the nature of the marriage decision in a model in which the agent may not get married at all. This possibility arises because the marrying agent's objective involves maximizing the *probability* of accepting the best possible marriage proposal, when these proposals are received sequentially. As we shall see, in this scenario, the marrying agent's optimal policy (OP) involves waiting a while and saying yes to the first marriage proposal thereafter.

The theory of optimal stopping[4] can be used to comprehend the nature of the marrying agent's choice problem. We now use this theory to formulate and analyze a model of decision making in arranged marriages.

3. THE THEORETICAL FRAMEWORK

The model is based on Gilbert and Mosteller (1966) and the spirit of the analysis is closely related to that in Batabyal (1998). Consider a stochastic environment in which our agent who seeks to be married receives marriage proposals sequentially in discrete time. The environment is stochastic because the decision to get married depends on the receipt of marriage proposals; these are of uncertain quality. It is assumed that successive marriage proposals are statistically independent. In other words, a particular marriage proposal is received at time t with a certain probability, independent of any previous or subsequent proposals. As discussed in section 2, this receipt of proposals is the result of investigative activities undertaken by the marring agent's family, friends, and intermediaries.

We shall first focus on the case of a known finite number—say n—of marriage proposals.[5] Upon receipt of a proposal, our marrying agent must decide whether to accept the proposal (say yes to marriage) or reject the proposal (say no to marriage) and wait for additional proposals. If the agent accepts a proposal, i.e., if he (or she) says yes to marriage, then the question of subsequent proposals is irrelevant. Consequently, the stochastic proposal generation process terminates. The agent's decision to say yes or no is binding in the sense that a rejected proposal cannot be recalled at a subsequent point in time.[6] Our marrying agent has no access to any prior information about the probabilistic nature of the proposals. Upon receipt of a proposal, the marrying agent is able to rank the proposal in terms of its quality. As such, the only information that the agent is privy to is the relative rank of a proposal, as compared to previous proposals. The marrying agent's objective is to maximize the probability of accepting the best (highest quality) marriage proposal when all $n!$ orderings of the various proposals are equally likely.

From the standpoint of the marrying agent, the scenario described above involves acting in a sequential decision making framework. We shall refer to a proposal as a candidate if this proposal is of higher rank (quality) than any previously received proposal. Further, we shall say that we are in state k, if the kth proposal, $1 \le k \le n$ has been received and it is a candidate. Let $W(k)$ denote the best decision that the marrying agent can make in this setting. Then it follows that

$$W(k) = \max \{P(k), R(k)], k = 1, \ldots, n, \qquad (3.1)$$

where $P(k)$ is the probability that the highest quality proposal will materialize if the kth proposal is accepted and $R(k)$ is the best decision that the agent can make if the kth proposal is rejected.[7] Now conditioning[8] on the event that the kth proposal is a candidate, we get

$$P(k) = P\{prop\ highest\ of\ n\ prop/prop\ highest\ of\ k\ prop\} = k/n \ . \tag{3.2}$$

An explicit interpretation can now be given to $R(k)$. It is the maximal probability of accepting the highest quality proposal when the previous k proposals have been rejected by our marrying agent. The reader should note that (i) $P(k)$ is increasing in k, and (ii) the case in which the first k proposals have been rejected is at least as desirable as the case in which the first $k + 1$ proposals have been rejected. These two facts tell us the $R(k)$ is decreasing in k. Now because $P(k)$ is increasing in k and $R(k)$ is decreasing in k, we know that there must exist a proposal l such that

$$k/n = P(k) \le R(k), \quad k \le l \tag{3.3}$$

and

$$k/n = P(k) > R(k), \quad k > l \tag{3.4}$$

hold. From equations (3.3) and (3.4), the nature of our marrying agent's optimal policy (hereafter OP) can be determined intuitively. This OP says the following: for some proposal $l \le n$ - 1, reject the first l proposals, i.e., say no to marriage, and then accept the first candidate proposal (say yes) received.

Having determined the nature of the marrying agent's OP, our next task is to compute the probability—$P_{OP}(highest)$—of accepting the marriage proposal of highest quality when this policy is used. From Ross (1993, p. 100), it follows that this probability is given by

$$P(highest) = \sum_{k=1}^{k=n-1} P_{OP}\{highest\ of\ n\ /\ k+1\ prop\ accepted\} \cdot$$
$$P_{OP}\{k+1\ prop\ accepted\}. \tag{3.5}$$

Now following the line of reasoning that led to equation (3.2), the conditional probability on the RHS of equation (3.5) can be simplified. This gives

$$P_{OP}\{highest\ of\ n/k+l\ prop\ accepted\} = (k + l)/n \ . \tag{3.6}$$

The second probability on the RHS of equation (3.5) can also be simplified by writing this probability as a joint probability. This simplification yields

$$P_{OP}\{k+l\ prop\ accepted\} = \{l/(k+l-1)\}\{1/(k+l)\} \ . \tag{3.7}$$

With equations (3.6) and (3.7), the expression for $P_{OP}(highest)$ in equation (3.5) can be written. This gives

$$P_{OP}(highest) = (l/n)\sum_{m=1}^{m=n-1}(1/m), \tag{3.8}$$

where $m = k + l - 1$. The probability in equation (3.8) is what our marrying agent wishes to maximize. However, in the finite n, i.e., the finite number of proposals case, this maximization exercise cannot be performed in any straightforward manner.[9] Hence, in what follows, we shall restrict attention to the asymptotic ($n \rightarrow \infty$) case.

For large n, the summand in equation (3.8) can be approximated well by the natural logarithm function. Using this approximation, we get

$$P_{OP}(highest) = (l/n)\log_e\{(n - 1)/l\} \ . \tag{3.9}$$

Let $h(z) \equiv (z/n)\log_e\{(n - 1)/z\} = P_{OP}(highest)$. Our marrying agent's optimization problem can now be stated. This agent solves

$$\max_z[(z/n)\log_e\{(n - 1)/z\}] \ . \tag{3.10}$$

The first-order necessary condition is

$$z^* = (n - 1)/e \ . \tag{3.11}$$

Substituting z^* into $h(\cdot)$ gives

$$h(z^*) = \{(n - 1)/n\}(1/e) \ . \tag{3.12}$$

Equation (3.12) gives us a quantitative characterization of the marring agent's OP. In turn, this leads to

Theorem 1: *The marrying agent should reject the first ($1/e$) fraction of marriage proposals and he (or she) should accept the first candidate's proposal thereafter.*[10]

Theorem 1 provides an answer to the "When to say yes" question. This theorem tells us that when faced with the prospect of receiving a large number of proposals sequentially, our marrying agent should initially say no to marriage, i.e., he (or she) should reject the first ($1/e$) fraction of all proposals. He (or she) should then say yes to the first candidate proposal. The probability that the use of this OP will result in the best proposal being accepted is $(1/e) = 0.37$. This tells us that irrespective of how actively friends, family, and intermediaries look for marriage proposals, if our marrying agent insists on saying yes only to the highest quality proposal, he (or she) may never get married at all.

To intuitively see why an OP of the type described in Theorem 1 makes sense, recall the irreversibility of the marriage decision. This irreversibility implies that there is an asymmetry associated with the marrying agent's yes/no decision. From the perspective of this agent, a no decision always leads to future options, but a yes decision terminates the stochastic proposal generation process. Consequently, there is a premium associated with a no decision because this decision preserves flexibility. The policy described in Theorem 1 optimally trades off this flexibility premium with the likelihood that the highest quality proposal will be lost if the agent waits too long to say yes.[11]

Consider the issue of the robustness of Theorem 1. In this connection, let us note that the only two assumptions that we needed to obtain the result described in this theorem are (i) that the marrying agent knows the relative rank of each marriage proposal, and (ii) that the successive marriage proposals be statistically independent. The informational assumption is parsimonious and the independence assumption is quite standard. Consequently, it seems reasonable to say that these two assumptions comprise the minimal set of assumptions that is necessary to generate the result contained in Theorem 1.

Now suppose that these assumptions do not hold. The independence assumption is clearly crucial; if this does not hold, then Theorem 1 will also not hold and the underlying problem will become substantially more complicated. While the marrying agent must have access to some information for his (or her) decision problem to be well-posed, the exact form of the informational assumption is not that important. For instance, suppose that our marrying agent is not privy to the relative rank of a proposal. Instead, this agent only observes numerical scores from some distribution function. As long as these scores are independent and the distribution from which the scores are drawn is known to the agent, Theorem 1 will continue to hold.

4. CONCLUSIONS

In this chapter we modeled the marriage decision in a dynamic and stochastic framework. In this setting, in response to the "When to say yes" question, we provided an OP for our marrying agent. This policy involved a probabilistic comparison of the benefit from accepting a current proposal, i.e., saying yes now, with the benefit to be obtained by rejecting the current proposal and waiting for future marriage proposals. The asymptotic optimality of this policy tells us that the policy is best viewed as an optimal course of action over a long time horizon—such as a lifetime—during which our marrying agent can be expected to receive a large number of marriage proposals.

The analysis of this chapter can be generalized in a number of directions. In what follows, we suggest two possible extensions. First, one can extend the analysis of this chapter by studying arranged marriage situations in which the marrying agent's role is not definitive but only consultative. This will involve the analysis of a different kind of stopping problem. Second, suppose that the marrying agent learns the statistical properties of the stochastic proposal generation process. We would then have a dynamic problem with an element of inference as well as of decision. In this situation, one can analyze scenarios in which the marrying agent first goes through a period of learning and then he (or she) makes a decision. A study of these aspects of the problem will permit richer analyses of the connections between the information gathering activities of family and friends and the marriage decision in an arranged marriage context.

REFERENCES

Auboyer, J. *Daily Life in Ancient India*. New York: Macmillan Press, 1965.

Batabyal, A.A. "Aspects of Arranged Marriages and the Theory of Markov Decision Processes." *Theory and Decision* 45 (1998): 241-53.

Becker, G.S. "A Theory of Marriage: Part I." *Journal of Political Economy* 81 (1973): 813-46.

———. *A Treatise on the Family*, enlarged ed. Cambridge, Mass.: Harvard University Press, 1991.

Dixit, A.K., and R.S. Pindyck. *Investment Under Uncertainty*. Princeton, N.J.: Princeton University Press, 1994.

Gilbert, J.P., and R. Mosteller. "Recognizing the Maximum of a Sequence." *Journal of the American Statistical Association* 61 (1966): 35-73.

Goode, W.J. *World Revolution and Family Patterns*. New York: Free Press, 1963.

Harris, M. *Dynamic Economic Analysis*. New York: Oxford University Press, 1987.

Mace, D., and V. Mace. *Marriage: East and West*. Garden City, N.Y.: Doubleday and Company, 1964.

Mandelbaum, D.G. *Society in India*. Berkeley: University of California Press, 1970.

McDonald, R., and D. Siegel. "The Value of Waiting to Invest." *Quarterly Journal of Economics* 101 (1986): 707-28.

Moore, M. "Changing India, Wedded to Tradition: Arranged Marriages Persist With 90s Twists." *Washington Post*, 8 October 1994.

Otani, K. "Distributions in the Process to Marriage and Pregnancy in Japan." *Population Studies* 45 (1991): 473-87.

Pindyck, R.S. "Irreversibility, Uncertainty, and Investment." *Journal of Economic Literature* 29 (1991): 1110-52.

Rao, V.V.P., and V.N. Rao. *Marriage, the Family and Women in India*. New Delhi, India: South Asia Books, 1982.

Ross, S.M. *Introduction to Probability Models*, 5th ed. San Diego, Cal.: Academic Press, 1993.

Vatuk, S. *Kinship and Urbanization: White Collar Migrants in North India*. Berkeley: University of California Press, 1972.

NOTES

1. See Mandelbaum (1970), Moore (1994), Otani (1991), and Rao and Rao (1982), for a more detailed corroboration of this claim.
2. For a more detailed description of the marriage-related investigative activities of parents, friends, and intermediaries, see Mace and Mace (1960) and Vatuk (1972).

3. By making this assumption we wish to capture the fact that in most societies in which arranged marriages are prevalent, social pressures are such that once the agent agrees to a marriage proposal, it is generally difficult for him (or her) to renege on the original decision, at least in the short run. We do not wish to imply that separation or divorce is never an option for the agent. Further, the reader should note that while the marrying agent's role described here is increasingly the prevalent one, it is not the only possible one. In some settings, the agent's role is essentially consultative. For more on this, see section 4.

4. For more on this, see Dixit and Pindyck (1994) and Harris (1987).

5. The asymptotic case, i.e., the $n \to \infty$ case, will be analyzed later.

6. For a detailed analysis of the effects of recall on the decision to say yes in an arranged marriage, see Batabyal (1998).

7. In all the subsequent equations of this chapter, highest means of highest quality, or alternately, of highest rank.

8. For more on this, see Ross (1993, pp. 100-06).

9. In the finite n case, one can provide approximations that give us lower and upper bounds on the optimal proposal that should be accepted by the marring agent. For more on this and related numerical approaches, see Gilbert and Mosteller (1966, pp. 36-40).

10. This statement uses the fact that $\lim_{n \to \infty}\{(n - 1)/n\} = 1$.

11. This is related to the "value of waiting" result in the investment under uncertainty literature. For more on this, see McDonald and Siegel (1986), Pindyck (1991), and Dixit and Pindyck (1994).

CHAPTER 4—
ON DECISION MAKING IN ARRANGED MARRIAGES WITH A STOCHASTIC RESERVATION QUALITY LEVEL

ABSTRACT

Recently, Batabyal (1999) has shown that when the decision to get married in an arranged marriage is analyzed in an intertemporal and stochastic setting, it is possible that a marrying agent will never get married. This result arises because the marrying agent in Batabyal (1999) maximizes the probability of accepting the best possible marriage proposal. What happens when a marrying agent uses the following decision rule: Get married as long as the quality of a marriage proposal exceeds a stochastic reservation quality level? In this chapter, we provide an interesting answer to this question. First, we show that the probability of getting married with this decision rule is always positive. Even so, we point out that on average, an agent who uses this decision rule will end up single.

Key words: arranged marriage, dynamics, reservation quality level, uncertainty

1. INTRODUCTION

Arranged marriages are predicated on the supposition that because of a variety of reasons such as imperfect and incomplete information (Goode 1963, p. 210) and the tendency of young people to seek pleasure (Auboyer 1965, p. 176), young persons generally cannot be relied upon to find an apposite spouse for themselves.[1] Therefore, parents, relatives, friends, and increasingly matchmaking intermediaries (hereafter well-wishers), take upon themselves the task of looking for a suitable bride or groom. Whereas in western societies, the agent wishing to marry generally looks for a spouse himself or herself, in an arranged marriage this crucial task is generally not undertaken by the agent but by his or her well-wishers.[2] The reader should note that this is a basic difference between arranged marriages and marriages in western countries.

The second pertinent feature of arranged marriages concerns the marrying agent's decision. As Blood (1967, p. 55), Rao and Rao (1982, pp. 32-33), and Applbaum (1995) have noted, in modern arranged marriage settings, the agent wishing to marry has considerable autonomy over the actual marriage decision. In the words of Blood (1967, p. 11), while well-wishers look for suitable marriage prospects, the agent is "given an explicit opportunity to veto the nominee before negotiations are pursued." This agent receives marriage proposals as a result of the exploratory activities (newspaper advertisements, phone calls, conversations with acquaintances) undertaken by his or her well-wishers. The marrying agent's problem is to decide (i) what kind of decision rule to use and (ii) which marriage proposal to say yes to.

Even though arranged marriages have been around for quite some time, economists have been interested in systematically studying marriages only since Becker (1973). Further, this interest has almost completely been confined to the study of marriages in western societies in a deterministic setting. As a result, even though the decision to get married in an arranged marriage has everything to do with decision making under uncertainty, we know very little about the stochastic properties of alternate decision rules in arranged marriages. Recently, Batabyal (1998, 1999, 2001) has analyzed stochastic models of decision making in arranged marriages. Using the so called one stage look ahead policy (OSLAP), Batabyal (1998) shows that a marrying agent's optimal decision rule depends only on the nature of the current marriage proposal, independent of whether there is recall of previous proposals. In Batabyal (2001), decision making in arranged marriages with an explicit age constraint is studied. In this setting, Batabyal (2001) shows that it is optimal to wait a while before saying yes to a marriage proposal. The fact that it is optimal to wait a while is consistent with the "value of waiting to invest" result in the investment under uncertainty literature.[3]

The Batabyal (1999) paper is the closest to our chapter. In that paper, the "When do I say yes to a marriage proposal" question is answered by analyzing the decision problem faced by a marrying agent who wishes to maximize "the *probability* of accepting the best possible marriage proposal, when these proposals are received sequentially" (Batabyal, 1999, p. 440, italics in original). In particular, it is shown that it may be optimal for the marrying agent to never say yes to a proposal, i.e., to never get married. The reader should note that this result has nothing to do with the marrying agent's time (and decision making) horizon. Rather, it arises because the marrying agent's optimization problem involves the maximization of a probability.

What happens when a marrying agent uses the following decision rule: Get married as long as the quality of a marriage proposal exceeds a stochastic reservation quality level? The objective of this chapter is to answer this hitherto unstudied question. As we shall see, in an intertemporal and stochastic setting, a rather interesting result arises and that result is this: The probability of getting married with this decision rule is always positive. However, in an expected waiting time sense, our marrying agent will have to wait an infinite amount of time before (s)he gets married. The remainder of this chapter is organized as follows: Section 2 provides a detailed discussion of the theoretical framework and the results. Section 3 concludes and offers suggestions for future research.

2. THE THEORETICAL FRAMEWORK

Consider an individual who wishes to get married in an arranged marriage. In what follows, we shall refer to this individual as our marrying agent. As a result of the investigative activities of this marrying agent's well-wishers, marriage proposals are brought to him or her sequentially in accordance with some independently and identically distributed (i.i.d.) stochastic process. In other words, a marriage proposal of some quality is received in time period t with a certain probability, independent of preceding or subsequent proposals. These proposals are received over time, one proposal per time period.

Looked at along the time dimension, the decision problem faced by our marrying agent concerns when (if ever) to say yes to a proposal. Alternately, looked at along the proposal dimension, this agent's decision problem concerns which proposal (if any) to say yes to. Following Batabyal (1999), we now make two assumptions. First, we suppose that the decision to say yes to a marriage proposal is binding in the sense that a previously rejected proposal cannot be recalled at a subsequent point in time.[4] Second, we suppose that a decision to say yes to a marriage proposal is irreversible. In other words, the possibility of divorce is disallowed and we are analyzing the marriage decision as a once in a lifetime decision.[5] The marrying agent solves his or her decision problem in an intertemporal and stochastic setting.

Upon receipt of a proposal, our marrying agent must decide whether to say yes to the proposal (get married) or to decline the proposal (stay unmarried) and wait for further proposals. If the marrying agent accepts a proposal, i.e., if (s)he says yes to marriage, then the question of subsequent proposals is redundant. Therefore, the stochastic marriage proposal receipt process terminates. We now need to specify a decision rule for our marrying agent. A simple decision rule—and the one we analyze in this chapter—is the following: Let $M_0, M_1, M_2, M_3, \ldots$ be i.i.d, nonnegative random variables that denote the quality of the marriage proposals that are received sequentially over time. In other words, M_0 is the quality of the first marriage proposal, M_1 is the quality of the second marriage proposal, and so on and so forth. We suppose that our marrying agent's (stochastic) reservation utility level is M_0, the quality of the first marriage proposal. Then, our marrying agent's decision rule is to accept the first proposal that exceeds M_0 in quality.

From the perspective of our marrying agent, the situation described in the previous two paragraphs involves acting in a sequential decision making framework. To this end, denote the common and the continuous distribution and the density functions of the random $M_0, M_1, M_2, M_3, \ldots$ marriage proposals by $G(\cdot)$ and $g(\cdot)$, respectively. Now, given our marrying agent's decision rule (see the previous paragraph), let N be the first index i for which $M_i > M_0$. In other words, $N = 1$ if $M_1 > M_0$, $N = 2$ if $M_1 \leq M_0$ and $M_2 > M_0$, and so on. Put differently, N is an index for the first proposal whose quality level exceeds the reservation quality level M_0. As an example, if $N = 30$, then looked at in terms of the waiting period, our marrying agent has to wait 29 time periods—recall that a proposal is received every time period—before (s)he says yes to a marriage proposal. Looked at in terms of the number of rejected proposals, our marrying agent turns down twenty-nine proposals and then says yes to the thirtieth marriage proposal.

Now, to comprehend the nature of the arranged marriage decision in the setting of this chapter, let us first compute the probability mass function $Prob\{N = n\}$ for the positive and integer valued random variable N. The computation of this probability mass function is facilitated by noting that $Prob\{N = n\} = Prob\{N > n - 1\} - Prob\{N > n\}$. Now, $Prob\{N > n\} = Prob\{M_0 \text{ is the largest among } (M_0, \ldots, M_n)\} = 1/(n + 1)$ because each random variable $M_j, j = 0, \ldots, n$, has the same chance of being the largest. More formally, we have

$$Prob\{N > n\} = \int_0^\infty [1 - G(m)]^n g(m)\, dm = -\int_0^\infty [1 - G(m)]^n d[1 - G(m)]. \qquad (4.1)$$

Now substitute $z = [1 - G(m)]$ in the right-most integral in equation (4.1). This gives

$$Prob\{N > n\} = \int_0^1 z^n dz = \frac{1}{n+1}. \qquad (4.2)$$

By using equation (4.2) we can infer that

$$Prob\{N = n\} = Prob\{N > n-1\} - Prob\{N > n\} = \frac{1}{n} - \frac{1}{n+1} = \frac{1}{n(n+1)}. \qquad (4.3)$$

Equation (4.3) gives us the probability mass function for the random variable N. Looking at equation (4.3), we see four interesting characteristics of the arranged marriage decision. First, for any finite N, the probability of saying yes to a marriage proposal (getting married) is always positive. Second, the maximal likelihood of getting married is ½ and this probability occurs when $N = 1$. Third, as N rises, the probability of getting married falls over time. Finally, in the limit as $N \to \infty$, the likelihood of getting married is zero. Together, these four characteristics tell us that the likelihood of getting married is higher early in the marrying agent's time and decision making horizon. This finding is consistent with reality. As noted in Blood (1967), Mullatti (1992), and Batabyal (2001), *ceteris paribus*, it is more difficult for an older agent to get married via the arranged marriage route.

So far we have seen that, for all practical purposes, i.e., for all finite N, the probability of getting married is positive. However, what is the expected wait time before our marrying agent is able to say yes to a proposal? Specifically, given the limiting result of the previous paragraph, is it possible that in an expected waiting time sense our marrying agent will never get married? To answer these questions, we now compute the mathematical expectation of N, $E[N]$. Because N is a nonnegative and integer valued random variable, we can use equation (4.2) and equation (5.2) in Taylor and Karlin (1998, p. 44)[6] to compute its expectation. We get

$$E[N] = \sum_{n=1}^\infty Prob\{N \geq n\} = \sum_{n=0}^\infty Prob\{N > n\} = \sum_{n=0}^\infty \frac{1}{n+1} = \infty. \qquad (4.4)$$

Equation (4.4) answers the two questions posed in the previous paragraph. Specifically, we see that even though the probability of getting married for all finite N is positive, the expected wait until marriage is *infinity*. Therefore, in an expected waiting time sense, our marrying agent will never say yes to a marriage proposal (always stay unmarried).

Batabyal (1999) showed that when a marrying agent maximizes the probability of accepting the best marriage proposal, it is possible that (s)he will never say yes to a proposal (never get married). Our equation (4.4) result complements the Batabyal (1999) finding. In particular, this result tells us that even when a marrying agent's focus is not on maximizing the probability of accepting the best marriage proposal, the use of the decision rule described in this chapter along with the *stochastic* reservation quality level can still tilt—in an expected waiting time sense—a marrying agent's decision in the direction of no arranged marriage. Further, the analysis of this chapter tells us that the decision rule analyzed here is sub-optimal in the sense that on average, a marrying agent following this rule will end up single.

Does the equation (4.4) result hold when our marrying agent's reservation quality level is deterministic and not stochastic? Our ongoing research on this subject tells us that the answer to this question is no. In other words, when the reservation quality level is fixed, the expected wait time until marriage is finite.

3. CONCLUSIONS

In this chapter we analyzed the arranged marriage decision in an intertemporal and stochastic framework. We used this framework to answer a previously unstudied question. What happens when a marrying agent uses the following decision rule: Get married as long as the quality of a marriage proposal exceeds a stochastic reservation quality level? Our analysis showed that for all finite N, the likelihood of getting married is always positive. Even so, in an expected waiting time sense, our marrying agent will have to wait infinitely long before (s)he is married. It is in this sense that our marrying agent ends up never getting married.

The analysis of this chapter can be extended in a number of directions. In what follows, we suggest two possible extensions. First, instead of working with an i.i.d. stochastic process, one could analyze the decision to get married in an arranged marriage in a setting in which the stochastic proposal receipt process exhibits serial correlation over time. Second, if the marrying agent learns about the statistical properties of the proposal receipt process, then it is possible that this agent will ultimately know the distribution from which the proposals are received. One could study the effects of this knowledge on the "Which proposal to say yes to" question. Studies that analyze these aspects of the problem will provide additional insights into the criteria that govern the decision to get married in an arranged marriage.

REFERENCES

Ahuvia, A.C., and M. Adelman, M. "Formal Intermediaries in the Marriage Market: A Typology and Review." *Journal of Marriage and the Family* 54 (1992): 452-463.

Applbaum, K.D. "Marriage with the Proper Stranger: Arranged Marriage in Metropolitan Japan." *Ethnology* 34 (1995): 37-51.

Auboyer, J. *Daily Life in Ancient India*. New York: Macmillan Press, 1965.

Batabyal, A.A. "Aspects of Arranged Marriages and the Theory of Markov Decision Processes." *Theory and Decision* 45 (1998): 241-253.

———. "A Dynamic and Stochastic Analysis of Decision Making in Arranged Marriages." *Applied Economics Letters* 6 (1999): 439-442.

———. "On the Likelihood of Finding the Right Partner in an Arranged Marriage." *Journal of Socio-Economics* 30 (2001): 273-280.

Becker, G.S. "A Theory of Marriage: Part I." *Journal of Political Economy* 81 (1973): 813-846.

———. *A Treatise on the Family*, enlarged edition. Cambridge: Harvard University Press, 1991.

Blood, R.O. *Love Match and Arranged Marriage: A Tokyo-Detroit Comparison*. New York: Free Press, 1967.

Dixit, A.K., and R.S. Pindyck. *Investment Under Uncertainty*. Princeton, N.J.: Princeton University Press, 1994.

Goode, W.J. *World Revolution and Family Patterns*. New York: Free Press, 1963.

Mace, D., and V. Mace. *Marriage: East and West*. Garden City, N.Y.: Doubleday and Company, 1960.

Mullatti, L. "Changing Profile of the Indian Family." In *The Changing Family in Asia*, edited by Y. Atal. Bangkok, Thailand: UNESCO, 1992.

Rao, V.V.P., and V.N. Rao. *Marriage, the Family and Women in India*. New Delhi, India: South Asia Books, 1982.

Taylor, H.M., and S. Karlin. *An Introduction to Stochastic Modeling*, 3rd ed. San Diego, Cal.: Academic Press, 1998.

Vatuk, S. *Kinship and Urbanization: White Collar Migrants in North India*. Berkeley: University of California Press, 1972.

NOTES

1. In the context of western societies, Becker (1991, p. 324) too has alluded to the significance of imperfect information in decision making.
2. For a more elaborate delineation of the marriage related activities of well-wishers, see Mace and Mace (1960), Blood (1967), Vatuk (1972), and Ahuvia and Adelman (1992).
3. For more on this literature, see Dixit and Pindyck (1994).
4. What happens when previously rejected proposals can be recalled is discussed in Batabyal (1998).

5. By making this assumption, we wish to capture the fact that in most societies in which arranged marriages are customary, social pressures are such that once the agent agrees to a marriage proposal, it is typically difficult for him or her to renege on the original decision, at least in the short run.

6. This equation provides a compact formula for computing upper tail probabilities of nonnegative and integer valued random variables.

CHAPTER 5—
SPOUSE SELECTION IN ARRANGED MARRIAGES: AN ANALYSIS OF TIME INVARIANT AND TIME VARIANT DECISION RULES

with Hamid Beladi

ABSTRACT

Even though arranged marriages have been around for quite a while, the economics literature has paid scant attention to the nature of decision making in such marriages. Consequently, very little is known about the effects of alternate decision rules on the spouse selection question in arranged marriages. Given this state of affairs, our chapter has three objectives. First, we construct a simple model of decision making in arranged marriages. Second, we use this model to analyze the expected utility of a marrying agent when this agent uses, respectively, time invariant and time variant decision rules. Finally, we compare and contrast the properties of time invariant and time variant decision rules and we discuss the magnitude of the premium arising from the maintenance of temporal flexibility in decision making.

Key words: arranged marriage, decision making, time invariant, time variant, uncertainty

1. INTRODUCTION

Arranged marriages have been around for quite some time and they have certainly stood the test of time. Even today, a nontrivial proportion of all marriages in large parts of Africa, Asia, and the Middle East, are arranged.[1] Therefore, social scientists in general and anthropologists and sociologists in particular have sought to investigate the complexities of arranged marriages.[2] In fact, to celebrate 1994 as the international year of the family, the UNESCO commissioned an extensive study on the changing family in Asia (Atal 1992). Arranged marriages received a considerable amount of attention in this study. Despite the popularity of arranged marriages, economists have been interested in systematically studying marriages only since Becker (1973).[3] Further, this interest has been confined almost entirely to the study of marriage in western societies in a deterministic setting.

In western style "love marriages," the individual wishing to get married typically looks for a spouse himself or herself. In contrast, in eastern style "arranged marriages," the individual wishing to get married does not look for a spouse himself or herself. Instead, it is this individual's family members, friends, relatives, and increasingly matchmaking intermediaries who look for a spouse. As such and as noted in Batabyal (2001), decision making processes in western love marriages are different from those used in arranged marriages. However, beyond recognizing this elementary fact, economists have contributed precious little to our understanding of the nature of decision making in arranged marriages.

Given this state of affairs, our chapter has three objectives. First, we construct an elementary model of decision making in arranged marriages. This model is a stylized depiction of the decision making process that is common to arranged marriages in many parts of the world. Consequently, the reader should note that it is unlikely that our model will capture every aspect of decision making in a particular arranged marriage. Second, we use our model to shed light on a question that, to the best of our knowledge, has *not* been studied previously in the literature on arranged marriages. This question concerns the expected utility of a marrying agent when this agent is able to choose between *time invariant* and *time variant* decision rules. Finally, we compare and contrast the properties of time invariant and time variant decision rules and then we discuss the magnitude of the premium arising from the maintenance of temporal flexibility in decision making.[4]

The rest of this chapter is organized as follows: Section 2 provides a review of the literature and an overview of a decision making process that fits a wide variety of arranged marriages. Section 3 uses a theoretical model and provides a detailed analysis of the effects of time invariant and time variant decision rules on the expected utility of a marrying agent. Next, this section talks about the properties of time invariant and time variant decision rules and then comments on the magnitude of the premium arising from the maintenance of temporal flexibility in decision making. Section 4 first offers some concluding comments and then this section makes suggestions for future research on arranged marriages.

2. AN OVERVIEW OF ARRANGED MARRIAGES

Arranged marriages are predicated on the supposition that because of a variety of reasons such as imperfect and incomplete information (Goode 1963, p. 210), and the tendency of young people to seek pleasure (Auboyer 1965, p. 176), young persons generally cannot be relied upon to find an appropriate spouse for themselves.[5] Therefore, parents, relatives, friends, and increasingly matchmaking intermediaries (hereafter well-wishers), take upon themselves the task of looking for a suitable bride. As noted in section 1, in western societies, the agent wishing to marry generally looks for a spouse himself. However, in an arranged marriage this crucial task is generally not undertaken by the agent but by his well-wishers.[6] The reader should note that this is a basic difference between arranged marriages and marriages in western countries.

The second pertinent feature of arranged marriages concerns the marrying agent's decision. As Blood (1967, p. 55), Rao and Rao (1982, pp. 32-33), and

Applbaum (1995) have noted, in modern arranged marriage settings, the agent wishing to marry has considerable autonomy over the actual marriage decision. In the words of Blood (1967, p. 11), while well-wishers look for suitable marriage prospects, the agent is "given an explicit opportunity to veto the nominee before negotiations are pursued." This agent receives marriage proposals as a result of the exploratory activities (newspaper advertisements, phone calls, conversations with acquaintances) that are undertaken by his well-wishers. The agent's problem is to decide (i) what kind of decision rule to use and (ii) which marriage proposal to say yes to.

Recently, Batabyal (1998, 1999, 2001) has studied stochastic models of decision making in arranged marriages. Batabyal (1998) shows that a marrying agent's optimal decision rule depends only on the nature of the current marriage proposal, independent of whether there is a recall of previous proposals. In Batabyal (1999), it is shown that the marrying agent's optimal decision rule involves waiting a while, and saying yes to the first marriage proposal thereafter.

The reader should note that in both these papers, the marrying agent's decision problem is modeled in a way that precludes considerations of age at marriage. In other words, in both these papers, the marrying agent follows an optimal decision rule. However, in following this rule, the agent does not care *when* in his lifetime he gets married. This is at odds with known facts about arranged marriages. For instance, data for Japan discussed in Blood (1967), and for India discussed in Mullatti (1992), tell us that virtually all marriages are completed by the age of 35 for men and 30 for women. This suggests that when modeling the decision making process in arranged marriages, one ought to explicitly account for the fact that a marrying agent typically has in mind a particular age by which he would like to be married. Batabyal (2001) has studied decision making in arranged marriages with an explicit age constraint. Even in this setting, Batabyal (2001) shows that it is optimal to wait a while before saying yes to a marriage proposal.

Although these papers have advanced our understanding of the nature of decision making in arranged marriages, they have not studied the properties of *time variant* decision rules. Clearly, time varying decision rules are more realistic than are time invariant decision rules. Further, time varying rules allow a marrying agent to be flexible over the length of his decision making horizon. Finally, the use of such rules is salient because as Blood (1967), Moore (1994), Applbaum (1995) and others have noted, the criteria that are important in the spouse selection decision tend to change with the passage of time. Moreover, the above mentioned papers have also not conducted a comparative analysis of the relative merits of time invariant and time variant decision rules. Consequently, we now use the theory of optimal stopping[7] to construct and analyze a model of decision making in arranged marriages in a dynamic and stochastic framework.

3. THE THEORETICAL FRAMEWORK

3.1. The Model

In order to keep things from getting unduly complicated, in the rest of this chapter we shall choose units so that the numerical values of all the relevant variables and the distribution functions are drawn from the interval (0, 1]. Now, consider a marrying agent who has a one-to-one and strictly monotonic utility function that is defined over marriage proposals. This agent wishes to be married by time $T = 1$. To emphasize the salience of this age constraint, we assume that if the agent fails to get married by time $T = 1$, then his utility is zero. As indicated in the previous section, the agent's well-wishers engage in activities that result in the receipt of marriage proposals. These proposals P_1, P_2, P_3, ... are received in accordance with a Poisson process[8] with a fixed rate $\lambda = 1$. The proposals themselves are independent random variables that are uniformly distributed on the interval (0, 1]. Upon receipt of a proposal, our agent meets the person behind the proposal, and this meeting generates a certain level of utility. It is on the basis of this utility that our agent decides whether to accept or to reject a particular proposal. Note that because our marrying agent's one-to-one and strictly monotonic utility function maps marriage proposals to utility and because these proposals are uniformly distributed on (0, 1], the utilities U_1, U_2, U_3, ... themselves are also uniformly distributed random variables on the interval (0, 1].

There is an asymmetry associated with the binary choice accept/reject decision. If our agent rejects a particular proposal then he can always accept a later proposal as long as he accepts this proposal by time $T = 1$. In contrast, if our agent accepts a particular proposal (he gets married), then his well-wishers will not bring any more proposals to him and the stochastic proposal receipt process terminates. Put differently, a decision to reject a proposal preserves future options whereas a decision to accept a proposal does not.[9] The reader should note that this asymmetry and the age constraint together will play a fundamental role in our subsequent analysis.

In order to accomplish his objective of getting married by time $T = 1$, our marrying agent will need to use a decision rule. In this chapter we shall consider two types of decision rules. The first decision rule is the time invariant one and this rule is of the following type: Our agent decides on some threshold level of utility $\hat{U}$ that is *independent* of time. With this decision rule, our marrying agent will accept the first proposal whose utility exceeds $\hat{U}$. For example, using this time invariant decision rule, if our agent accepts the fourth proposal, then it is necessarily true that $U_1 \leq \hat{U}$, $U_2 \leq \hat{U}$, $U_3 \leq \hat{U}$, and $U_4 > \hat{U}$. The second decision rule is the time variant decision rule and in this case the threshold level of utility is itself a function of time t. In other words, instead of working with a fixed $\hat{U}$, our agent will now work with a *time dependent* threshold $\hat{U}(t)$, where $\hat{U}(t) = (1 - t)/(3 - t)$.

Before closing this section we should point out that time variant decision rules can be of various levels of complexity. Most of the more complex decision rules do not permit the researcher to obtain closed-form solutions. Consequently, in this chapter we have chosen to work with a relatively simple decision rule because it allows us to obtain closed-form solutions and because—consistent with our objectives—the use of this rule enables us to compare the effects of time invariant and time variant decision rules in a straightforward manner. We now proceed to our analysis of the time invariant decision rule.

3.2. The Time Invariant Decision Rule

Our goal in this section is to compute the expected utility of our agent when he uses a time invariant decision rule with utility threshold $\hat{U}$. To this end, let us first determine the probability of getting married by time $T = 1$ when this decision rule is used. Because the utility process deriving from the stochastic proposal receipt process is a Poisson process with rate $\lambda = 1$, we can tell that the probability that we seek is

$$Prob\{getting\,married\,by\,T = 1\} = 1 - \exp\{-(1 - \hat{U})\}. \tag{5.1}$$

Our next task is to determine the expected utility of the proposal that results in our agent getting married by time $T = 1$. Now recall that these utilities are uniformly distributed on the interval $(0, 1]$. Hence, given that our agent gets married by time $T = 1$, the expected utility of the proposal that results in marriage is $(1 + \hat{U})/2$. We can now determine our agent's expected utility EU_{TI} from marriage with a time invariant decision rule. This is given by multiplying $(1 + \hat{U})/2$ by the probability on the right-hand side (RHS) of equation (5.1). We get

$$EU_{TI} = \left[\frac{1 + \hat{U}}{2}\right]\left[1 - \exp\{-(1 - \hat{U})\}\right]. \tag{5.2}$$

Equation (5.2) tells us that when a time invariant decision rule is used, the expected utility from marriage is the product of two terms in square brackets. Both these terms in the square brackets contain the utility threshold $\hat{U}$. Note that equation (5.2) is also our marrying agent's objective function. Consequently, with this information in mind, we can now ask the following question: What value of the utility threshold $\hat{U}$ should our agent pick to maximize his expected utility from marriage? This question can be answered by letting our agent solve

$$\max_{\hat{U}}\left[\left[\frac{1 + \hat{U}}{2}\right]\left[1 - \exp\{-(1 - \hat{U})\}\right]\right] \tag{5.3}$$

This is a straightforward but tedious maximization problem. After several steps, the first-order necessary condition for a maximum can be written as

$$\log_e(2+\hat{U})+\hat{U}=1. \tag{5.4}$$

Because $\hat{U} \in (0,1]$, it is easy to see that the solution to equation (5.4) is given by $\hat{U}^* = 0.2079$. In other words, if our agent sets the value of the utility threshold $\hat{U}^* = 0.2079$, then he will have maximized his expected utility from marriage.

What is the maximized value of our agent's expected utility? This question can be answered by substituting $\hat{U}^* = 0.2079$ into equation (5.2). This tells us that our agent's maximized expected utility from marriage is

$$EU_{TI}^* = \left[\frac{1+\hat{U}^*}{2}\right]\left[1-\exp\{-(1-\hat{U}^*)\}\right] = 0.330425. \tag{5.5}$$

Equation (5.5) tells us that the expected utility to our marrying agent when he uses the optimal time invariant decision rule is 0.330425. Put differently, this is the highest level of expected utility that our agent can hope to attain with a time invariant decision rule. This state of affairs naturally leads to the following question: Can our marrying agent do better by using a time variant decision rule? We now proceed to answer this question.

3.3. The Time Variant Decision Rule

Our aim now is to compute the agent's expected utility from marriage when he uses a time variant decision rule of the form $\hat{U}(t) = (1 - t)/(3 - t)$. Proceeding in the same manner as in the previous section, let us first ascertain the likelihood of getting married by time $T = 1$ when the above time variant decision rule is used. Because the decision rule now is time variant, the likelihood that we are interested in can be determined by computing the probability of getting married in a small time interval $[t, t + dt]$. Using the properties of the Poisson process (see endnote 8), we have

$$Prob\{getting\ married\ within[t,t+dt]\}=\exp\{-\int_0^t(1-\hat{U}(s))ds\}\,\{1-\hat{U}(t)\}dt. \tag{5.6}$$

By comparing equations (5.1) and (5.6), we see that the time varying nature of the decision rule complicates the computation of the likelihood of marriage. We now need to calculate the expected utility of the proposal that results in our agent getting married by time $T = 1$. Once again following the logic of the previous section, we obtain a similar expression for this expected utility. Consequently, we can now determine our agent's expected utility EU_{TV} from marriage with a time variant decision rule. This is given by multiplying $(1 + \hat{U}(t))/2$ by the probability on the RHS of equation (5.6) and then integrating the resulting expression between 0 and

1. In symbols, we have

$$EU_{TV} = \int_0^1 \left[\frac{1+\hat{U}(t)}{2} \right] \exp\{-\int_0^t (1-\hat{U}(s))ds\} \{1-\hat{U}(t)\}dt. \tag{5.7}$$

Equation (5.7) tells us that when a time variant decision rule is used, the expected utility from marriage is the product of two terms. As in section 3.2, both these terms contain the utility threshold $\hat{U}(\cdot)$. Also, observe that equation (5.7) is our marrying agent's objective function. However, owing to the time varying nature of our agent's decision rule, we cannot now compute an optimal $\hat{U}^*$ as we did in the previous section.

This notwithstanding, we can still ask: What is the maximized value of our agent's expected utility when he uses a time variant decision rule? To answer this question, we will need to perform the integrations in equation (5.7). Let us first perform the integration in the expression for the probability of getting married in the interval $[t, t + dt]$, i.e., in the second term on the RHS of equation (5.7). This integration gives

$$\exp\{-\int_0^t (1-\hat{U}(s))ds\} \{1-\hat{U}(t)\} dt = \frac{1}{9}(\frac{2}{3-t}) \exp\{2\log_e(3-t)\}dt. \tag{5.8}$$

By using equation (5.8) we can substantially simplify the objective function described by equation (5.7). This simplification yields

$$EU_{TV} = \frac{2}{9} \int_0^1 (2-t)dt. \tag{5.9}$$

Now performing the integration in equation (5.9), we get

$$EU_{TV}^* = \frac{2}{9} \int_0^1 (2-t)dt = 0.333333. \tag{5.10}$$

Equation (5.10) tells us that the expected utility of our marrying agent when he uses a time variant decision rule is 0.333333. In other words, this is the highest level of expected utility that our agent can hope to attain with the time variant decision rule $\hat{U}(t) = (1 - t)/(3 - t)$. We now compare and contrast the properties of time invariant and time variant decision rules and then we discuss the magnitude of the premium arising from the maintenance of temporal flexibility in decision making.

3.4. Discussion

In principle, for reasons given in the next paragraph, we expect time invariant and time variant decision rules to yield very different payoffs to a marrying agent. Our analysis thus far permits us to shed light on this and related issues. In particular, we can use Table 5.1 to compare and contrast the properties of these two different decision rules. Reading horizontally, the second row of Table 5.1 reveals the basic difference in the two rules. In the time invariant case, the optimal value of the utility threshold $\hat{U}$ is fixed at 0.2079 and this value does *not* change with the passage of time. In contrast, when our marrying agent's decision rule is time variant, the utility threshold is *always* a function of time and hence its optimal value will typically change with the passage of time.

The third row of Table 5.1 gives us exact values of the expected utility from marriage when these two decision rules are used by our agent. Relative to a time invariant decision rule, a time variant decision rule permits a marrying agent to be flexible and, hence, adaptable in the face of changing circumstances. To see this more clearly, consider the following example: In this paper, we have chosen units so that the age constraint is $T = 1$. For the purpose of this example, let us measure time in years and let us suppose that the age constraint is $T = 35$ years. Then, following the discussion in the last paragraph of section 2, it is reasonable to say that the optimal value of $\hat{U}$ for our agent when he is 20 years old will most likely be different from the optimal value of $\hat{U}$ when this agent is 33 years old. Now, in contrast with a time invariant decision rule, the use of a time variant decision rule allows our marrying agent to alter the value of $\hat{U}$ over time and, hence, in general, this decision rule is more flexible and therefore more desirable. The third row of Table 5.1 shows that this line of thinking is correct because $EU^*_{TV} = 0.333333 > 0.330425 = EU^*_{TI}$.

How much more desirable is the time variant decision rule? The simple answer is: Not much more. As shown in the fourth row of Table 5.1, the premium associated with the maintenance of temporal flexibility—and hence adaptability—in decision making is positive but only 0.002908. Consequently, in the theoretical

Table 5.1. A Comparison of Time Invariant and Time Variant Decision Rules

Criterion of Interest	Time Invariant Decision Rule	Time Variant Decision Rule
Optimal Value of Utility Threshold	$\hat{U}^* = 0.2079$	$\hat{U}(t) = \dfrac{1-t}{3-t}$
Maximal Expected Utility from Marriage	$EU^*_{TI} = 0.330425$	$EU^*_{TV} = 0.333333$
Premium from the Maintenance of Temporal Flexibility	$EU^*_{TV} - EU^*_{TI} = 0.002908 > 0$	

framework of this chapter, our marrying agent does almost as well by using a time invariant decision rule. This result is most likely due to the fact that we have worked with a relatively simple time variant decision rule in this chapter. The use of more complicated time variant decision rules will probably increase the magnitude of this flexibility premium. However, the reader should note that as indicated toward the end of section 3.1, these more complicated time-variant decision rules generally do not admit closed-form solutions.

4. CONCLUSIONS

In this chapter we provided a theoretical analysis of the nature of decision making in arranged marriages. To the best of our knowledge, this is the *first* comparative analysis of the properties of time invariant and time variant decision rules in an arranged marriage context. After pointing out the basic difference between time invariant and time variant decision rules, our analysis showed that time variant decision rules are generally more desirable than time invariant decision rules because the expected utility from marriage when a time variant decision rule is used is higher than the expected utility from marriage with a time invariant decision rule. Put differently, there is a positive flexibility premium associated with the use of a time variant decision rule.

The analysis of this chapter can be extended in a number of directions. In what follows, we suggest two possible extensions. First, in order to capture the idea that marriage proposals are more likely to be received in certain time intervals in a marrying agent's lifetime, one can let the rate at which marriage proposals are received by our agent be a function of time. As indicated in endnote 8, this will involve the analysis of a non-homogeneous Poisson process with an intensity function, say, $\lambda(t)$, $t \geq 0$.

The time variant decision rule that we've analyzed in this chapter involves altering the *value* of the utility threshold. However, the *form* of the decision rule itself does not change. Consequently, it would be useful to compare and contrast the properties of the time variant decision rule of this chapter with a different decision rule that involves the temporal alteration of the form of the decision rule. A study of these aspects of the problem will permit richer analyses of the nexuses between alternate decision rules and a marrying agent's optimal stopping problem.

REFERENCES

Applbaum, K.D. "Marriage with the Proper Stranger: Arranged Marriage in Metropolitan Japan." *Ethnology* 34 (1995) 37-51.

Ahuvia, A.C., and M. Adelman. "Formal Intermediaries in the Marriage Market: A Typology and Review." *Journal of Marriage and the Family* 54 (1992): 452-463.

Atal, Y. (ed.). *The Changing Family in Asia*. Bangkok, Thailand: UNESCO, 1992.

Auboyer, J. *Daily Life in Ancient India.* New York: Macmillan Press, 1965.

Batabyal, A.A. "Aspects of Arranged Marriages and the Theory of Markov Decision Processes." *Theory and Decision* 45 (1998): 241-253.

———. "A Dynamic and Stochastic Analysis of Decision Making in Arranged Marriages." *Applied Economics Letters* 6 (1999): 439-442.

———. "On the Likelihood of Finding the Right Partner in an Arranged Marriage." *Journal of Socio-Economics* 30 (2001): 273-280.

Becker, G.S. "A Theory of Marriage: Part I." *Journal of Political Economy* 81 (1973): 813-846.

———. *A Treatise on the Family,* enlarged edition. Cambridge: Harvard University Press, 1991.

Blood, R.O. *Love Match and Arranged Marriage: A Tokyo-Detroit Comparison.* New York: Free Press, 1967.

Croll, E. *The Politics of Marriage in Contemporary China.* Cambridge, U.K.: Cambridge University Press, 1981.

Dixit, A.K., and R.S. Pindyck. *Investment Under Uncertainty.* Princeton: Princeton University Press, 1994.

Goode, W.J. *World Revolution and Family Patterns.* New York: Free Press, 1963.

Harris, M. *Dynamic Economic Analysis.* New York: Oxford University Press, 1987.

Kulkarni, V.G. *Modeling and Analysis of Stochastic Systems.* London: Chapman and Hall, 1995.

Lavely, W. "Marriage and Mobility Under Rural Collectivism." In *Marriage and Inequality in Chinese Society,* edited by R.S. Watson and P.B. Ebrey. Berkeley: University of California Press, 1991.

Mace, D., and V. Mace. *Marriage: East and West.* Garden City, N.Y.: Doubleday and Company, 1960.

Malhotra, A. "Gender and the Timing of Marriage: Rural-Urban Differences in Java." *Journal of Marriage and the Family* 59 (1997): 434-450.

Mandelbaum, D.G. *Society in India.* Berkeley: University of California Press, 1970.

Moore, M. "Changing India, Wedded to Tradition: Arranged Marriages Persist With 90s Twists." *Washington Post,* 8 October 1994.

Mullatti, L. "Changing Profile of the Indian Family." In *The Changing Family in Asia,* ed. Y. Atal. Bangkok, Thailand: UNESCO, 1992.

Otani, K. "Distributions in the Process to Marriage and Pregnancy in Japan." *Population Studies* 45 (1991): 473-487.

Rao, V.V.P., and V.N. Rao. *Marriage, the Family and Women in India.* New Delhi, India: South Asia Books, 1982.

Ross, S.M. *Introduction to Stochastic Dynamic Programming.* San Diego: Academic Press, 1983.

———. *Stochastic Processes,* 2nd edition. San Diego: Academic Press, 1996.

Turnbull, C.M. (ed.). *Africa and Change.* New York: Knopf, 1973.

Vatuk, S. *Kinship and Urbanization: White Collar Migrants in North India.* Berkeley: University of California Press, 1972.

Wolf, M. *Women and the Family in Rural Taiwan.* Stanford: Stanford University Press, 1972.

NOTES

1. For a more detailed corroboration of this claim, consult Goode (1963), Mandelbaum (1970), Rao and Rao (1982), Otani (1991), and Moore (1994).
2. For more on this literature, see Blood (1967), Wolf (1972), Turnbull (1973), Croll (1981), Lavely (1991), Atal (1992), Malhotra (1997), and Batabyal (2001).
3. For a more recent account of this line of work, see Becker (1991).
4. In the rest of this chapter, we shall conduct the analysis from the perspective of a male marrying agent. The analysis is identical for a female agent. Although our analysis, in principle, applies to male and to female marrying agents, in many arranged marriage settings, female marrying agents tend to have less bargaining power than male marrying agents.
5. In the context of marriages in western societies, Becker (1991, p. 324) too has alluded to the significance of imperfect information in decision making.
6. For a more elaborate delineation of the marriage related activities of well-wishers, see Mace and Mace (1960), Blood (1967), Vatuk (1972), and Ahuvia and Adelman (1992).
7. For textbook treatments of the theory of optimal stopping, see Ross (1982), Harris (1987), and Dixit and Pindyck (1994).
8. For lucid discussions of the Poisson process, see Kulkarni (1995, pp. 186-238) and Ross (1996, pp. 59-97). If the receipt of marriage proposals is bunched over time, i.e., if more proposals are received in certain time intervals and less in other time intervals, then we would model the marriage proposal receipt process with a non-homogenous Poisson process. See the previous two cited sources for additional details on this point.
9. A question that arises now concerns the fate of rejected proposals. In particular, should it be possible to recall a previously rejected proposal? Our reading of the relevant literature tells us that in most arranged marriage settings, it is normally not possible to recall previously rejected proposals. Further, Batabyal (1998) has already analyzed the effects of recall on the decision to say yes in an arranged marriage. Therefore, in the rest of this chapter, we disallow the possibility of recalling a previously rejected proposal.

CHAPTER 6—
ON THE LIKELIHOOD OF FINDING THE RIGHT PARTNER IN AN ARRANGED MARRIAGE

ABSTRACT

Although arranged marriages have been around for quite a while, the economics literature has paid scant attention to the nature of decision making in such marriages. Consequently, very little is known about the utility of traditional methods of decision making in arranged marriages. Given this state of affairs, this chapter has three objectives. First, we formalize the traditional decision making process in arranged marriages. We then analyze the properties of this formalized decision making process from the perspective of a marrying agent. Finally, once again from the perspective of a marrying agent, we study the likelihood that the use of this decision making process will result in the agent finding the right partner for himself or herself.

Key words: arranged marriage, decision making, uncertainty

1. INTRODUCTION

Arranged marriages have been around for quite a while. Not only has this form of marriage stood the test of time, even today in large parts of Africa, Asia, and the Middle East, a significant proportion of all marriages are arranged.[1] Consequently, social scientists of all stripes have sought to study the intricacies of arranged marriages.[2] In fact, to commemorate 1994 as the international year of the family, the UNESCO commissioned a large study on the changing family in Asia (Atal, 1992). Arranged marriages received a considerable amount of attention in this study. This popularity of arranged marriages notwithstanding, economists have been interested in systematically analyzing marriages only since Becker (1973). Further, this interest has largely been restricted to the study of marriage in western societies in a deterministic setting. The fact that decision making processes in western "love" marriages are different from those used in arranged marriages is not in dispute. However, beyond recognizing this simple fact, economists have contributed very little to our understanding of the nature of decision making in arranged marriages.

Given this state of affairs, this chapter has three objectives. First, we formalize the traditional decision making process in arranged marriages. The reader should note that this formalization is an attempt to capture those aspects of decision making that are common to arranged marriages in many different parts of the world. Consequently, it is unlikely that our formalization will capture every aspect of decision making in a specific arranged marriage. Second, we analyze the properties of this decision making process from the perspective of a marrying agent. Finally, once again from the perspective of a marrying agent, we study the likelihood that the use of this decision making process will result in the agent finding the right partner for himself or herself.[3]

The rest of this chapter is organized as follows: Section 2 provides a review of the literature and an overview of a decision making process that fits a wide variety of arranged marriages. Section 3 studies a formal model of decision making based on the discussion in section 2, and then compares the findings of this chapter with the extant literature on arranged marriages in anthropology and sociology. Section 4 concludes and offers suggestions for future research.

2. AN OVERVIEW OF ARRANGED MARRIAGES

Arranged marriages are based on the assumption that because of a variety of reasons such as imperfect and incomplete information (Goode, 1963, p. 210), and the tendency of young people to seek pleasure (Auboyer, 1965, p. 176), young persons generally cannot be relied upon to find a suitable partner for themselves.[4] Consequently, parents, relatives, friends, and increasingly matchmaking intermediaries (hereafter well-wishers), take upon themselves the task of looking for a suitable bride. While in western societies, the agent wishing to marry generally looks for a partner himself, in an arranged marriage this important task is generally *not* undertaken by the agent but by his well-wishers.[5] The reader should note that this is a fundamental difference between arranged marriages and marriages in western nations.

The second germane aspect of arranged marriages concerns the marrying agent's decision. As Blood (1967, p. 55), Rao and Rao (1982, pp. 32-33), and Applbaum (1995) have noted, in modern arranged marriage settings, the agent wishing to marry has considerable autonomy over the actual marriage decision. In the words of Blood (1967, p. 11), while well-wishers look for apposite marriage prospects, the agent is "given an explicit opportunity to veto the nominee before negotiations are pursued." This agent receives marriage proposals as a result of the investigative activities—such as the placement of newspaper advertisements—that are undertaken by his well-wishers. In essence, the agent's problem is to decide which marriage proposal to say yes to.

Recently, Batabyal (1998, 1999) has analyzed stochastic models of decision making in arranged marriages. Batabyal (1998) shows that a marrying agent's optimal policy depends only on the nature of the current marriage proposal, independent of whether there is recall of previous proposals. In Batabyal (1999), it is shown that the marrying agent's optimal policy involves waiting a while, and saying yes to the first marriage proposal thereafter.

In both these papers, the marrying agent's decision problem is modeled in a way that precludes considerations of age at marriage. Put differently, in these papers, the marrying agent follows an optimal policy; however, in following this policy the agent does not care *when* in his lifetime he gets married. This is at odds with empirical facts. For instance, data for Japan discussed in Blood (1967), and for India discussed in Mullatti (1992), suggest that virtually all marriages are completed by the age of 35 for men and 30 for women. Given this situation, an objective of this chapter is to explore the generality of some of Batabyal's previous results, when the marrying agent has in mind a specific age by which he would like to be married.

The theory of optimal stopping can be used to study the marrying agent's choice problem.[6] Consequently, we now use this theory to formulate and analyze a model of decision making in arranged marriages.

3. THE THEORETICAL FRAMEWORK

3.1. The Model

Consider an agent who wishes to be married by a particular age, say T years of age. This agent has a utility function that is defined over marriage proposals. The utility function consists of a deterministic part and an additive stochastic part. The deterministic part is known to the marrying agent *and* to his well-wishers. The additive stochastic part is known *only* to the marrying agent. This is intended to capture the idea that well-wishers generally have a good but not perfect idea about the agent's preferences regarding his choice of marriage partner. As indicated in the previous section, the agent's well-wishers engage in activities that result in the receipt of marriage proposals. We suppose that these proposals are received in accordance with a Poisson process[7] with a fixed rate β Upon receipt of a proposal, these well-wishers bring this proposal to the marrying agent.

When a proposal is brought to the agent, this agent can either say yes to the proposal or reject it and wait for additional proposals. If a particular proposal is rejected by the agent, then his well-wishers will bring a subsequent proposal to the agent only if they believe this proposal to be of higher quality. Further, our marrying agent knows that his well-wishers will act in this manner. Consequently, in a stochastic sense, the marrying agent's objective is to say yes to the last proposal that is received before time T. To see this, recall that our agent's total utility is the sum of the deterministic part, which is known to the agent and to his well-wishers, and the stochastic part, which is known only to the agent. Consequently, this agent's total utility is a monotonically increasing function of his deterministic utility. It is in this sense that the last proposal is the right proposal.

Now suppose that in order to accomplish this objective, our marrying agent decides to wait a while, and then say yes to the first proposal that is brought to him.[8] Is this a desirable strategy? How long should the agent wait before saying yes? In particular, if our agent uses this strategy, what is the likelihood that he will accomplish his objective? These are the questions that remain to be answered. However, before we answer these questions, let us first discuss the tradeoff that confronts our agent.

If this agent acts too quickly and says yes to a proposal that is brought to him at time t, $t\epsilon[0,T]$, and a subsequent proposal could have been brought to him in the interval $(t,T]$, then the agent will not have made the best possible choice. On the other hand, if the marrying agent rejects proposals and waits too long, and no additional proposals are brought to him by time T, then the agent will have failed in his mission to be married by the time he is T years of age.

A question that arises now concerns the fate of rejected proposals. More specifically, should it be possible to recall a previously rejected proposal? Our reading of the relevant literature tells us that in most arranged marriage settings, it is normally not possible to recall previously rejected proposals. Further, Batabyal (1998) has already analyzed the effects of recall on the decision to say yes in an arranged marriage. Consequently, in what follows, we disallow the possibility of recalling a previously rejected proposal. Let us now answer the questions that were posed at the end of an earlier paragraph.

Suppose our agent decides to wait for w units of time, before saying yes to a marriage proposal that is brought to him. Obviously, $w\epsilon[0,T]$. Our task now is to express the agent's objective mathematically. Recall that if a particular proposal is rejected by the agent, then his well-wishers will bring a subsequent proposal to the agent only if they believe the proposal to be of higher utility. This means that the probability of being successful with the above described strategy is equal to the probability that only a single proposal is brought to the agent in the time interval $[w,T]$. This probability equals

$$Prob\ \{1\ proposal \in [w,T]\} = \beta(T-w)\exp\{-\beta(T-w)\}. \qquad (6.1)$$

Having determined the probability of being successful with the above-described strategy, our next task is to determine the length of the optimal waiting period for our marrying agent. This length, w^*, is the solution to

$$\max_w \beta(T-w)\exp\{\beta(T-w)\}. \qquad (6.2)$$

Now, differentiating equation (6.2) with respect to w, the first-order necessary condition to this maximization problem is[9]

$$w^* = T - \tfrac{1}{\beta}. \qquad (6.3)$$

Equation (6.3) tells us that the length of the optimal waiting period equals the age by which our agent would like to be married less the reciprocal of the rate at which marriage proposals are received by the agent's well-wishers.[10]

3.2. Discussion

We can now perform some comparative static exercises to determine the impact of changes in β and T on w^*. Holding β constant and differentiating equation (6.3) with respect to T, we see that $dw^*/dT = 1 > 0$. This tells us that all else being equal, an increase in the age by which our agent would like to be married has the effect of lengthening the period of time for which it is optimal to wait before saying yes to a marriage proposal. Similarly, if we keep T fixed and differentiate equation (6.3) with respect to β, we get $dw^*/d\beta = (1/2\beta) > 0$. Like in the previous case, this tells us that, *ceteris paribus*, if the rate at which the agent's well-wishers receive proposals increases, then too it is optimal for this agent to wait longer before accepting a marriage proposal.

If we think of marriage as an investment decision, then the analysis thus far confirms the wisdom of the "value of waiting to invest" result from the investment under uncertainty literature.[11] In particular, our analysis tells us that the optimal course of action for an agent who wishes to have an arranged marriage by the time he is T years of age, involves waiting a while, and then saying yes to the proposal that is brought to him. We are now in a position to answer the question that is implicit in the title of this paper: What is the likelihood of finding the best partner? To answer this question, let us substitute the expression for the optimal waiting time, w^*, from equation (6.3) into equation (6.1). This gives us the required probability; this probability is $(1/e) = 0.37$. This tells us that the cooperation of well-wishers, combined with the pursuit of an optimal strategy will enable our marrying agent to do quite well in finding the right partner in an arranged marriage.

To intuitively see why a strategy of the type that we have been analyzing so far makes sense, note that there is an asymmetry associated with the marrying agent's accept/reject decision. From the perspective of this agent, a decision to reject a proposal leads (stochastically) to future options, but a decision to accept a proposal does not. Consequently, there is a premium associated with a decision to reject a proposal because this decision preserves flexibility. The strategy that we have been analyzing optimally trades off this flexibility premium with the probability that the best proposal will be lost if the agent waits too long to accept a marriage proposal.

3.3. Our Results and the Related Literature

This chapter makes a claim and then presents three results about arranged marriages. The claim is that in general, marrying agents wish to get married by a certain age, say T. Consequently, it is important to account for this explicitly in theoretical models of arranged marriages. Our first result is that it is optimal to wait a while before saying yes to a marriage proposal. Our second result says that when T increases, it is optimal to wait longer before saying yes to marriage. Our third and final result says that when β (the rate at which marriage proposals are received) increases, it is once again optimal to wait longer before saying yes to marriage.

How do these results compare with the extant literature on arranged marriages in anthropology and sociology? To answer this question, let us address the claim and each result in turn. There is abundant support for the claim. For instance, Mullatti (1992, pp. 93-98) notes that in India, although the mean age at marriage has been rising over time, almost all marriages for both men and women are completed by the age of 35. Chowdhury (1992, pp. 52-55) points out that this is true in the case of Bangladesh as well. As a third example, consider the case of Japan. Here, Applbaum (1995, p. 47) points to the importance of the "proper marriageable age" by discussing the case of a representative women by the name of Hiroko. Hiroko points out that it is important for her to get married by the age of 30.

For countries in which arranged marriages are prevalent, we can determine whether there is empirical support for our first result by checking to see whether most marriages occur close to or some years away from the legal minimum age for marriage. Chowdhury (1992, p. 52) tells us that the "effective" minimum age for marriage in Bangladesh is 14 for females and 18 for males.[12] This notwithstanding, since 1974, the mean age at marriage for males has been 23.9 years or higher and for females it has been 15.9 years or higher. The story is similar in China. Croll (1981, p. 60) notes that Article 980 of the Family Law of 1931 made 18 and 16 the legal minimum age for marriage for males and females respectively. Nevertheless, most young people and their role models "wait until their late twenties or early thirties to initiate marriage negotiations . . ." (Croll, 1981, p. 70). These examples tell us that there is some support for the result that it is optimal to wait a while before saying yes to marriage.

Our second result says that as T goes up, the optimal waiting period increases. Although it is difficult to find evidence that directly supports this result, there is indirect evidence that supports the result. In many countries in which arranged marriages are commonplace, governments have been actively attempting to raise T. One can ask what impact these attempts have had on the waiting period before marriage. In some countries at least, the answer is that these attempts have succeeded in *raising* the waiting period. The evidence is perhaps clearest in the case of China. As noted by Croll (1981, p. 69, pp. 77-78), in Jiang village, attempts by the Chinese government to raise T have resulted in a steady increase in the mean age at marriage for both men and women; from 22.1 years in the 1950s to 26.3 years in the 1970s for men and from 21.1 years in the 1950s to 24.4 years in the 1970s for women. In other words, in accordance with our second result, $dw^*/dT > 0$.

To the best of our knowledge, the specific question as to what impact the rate at which marriage proposals are received—either by a marrying agent or by his well-wishers—has on the optimal waiting period has not been studied previously by anthropologists and sociologists. Consequently, we are not aware of any evidence that either supports or contradicts our third result that $dw^*/d\beta > 0$. We now discuss this issue in the next section.

4. CONCLUSIONS

In this chapter we formalized the traditional decision making process in arranged marriages. This formalization led us to study the properties of this decision making process in a dynamic and stochastic framework. *A la* Batabyal (1999), our analysis demonstrates the desirability of using strategies that call for waiting first, and then acting. In the context of this chapter, we showed that the optimal strategy for an agent who wishes to have an arranged marriage by the time he is *T* years of age, involves waiting a while and then saying yes to the proposal that is brought to him. In particular, this strategy involves a probabilistic comparison of the benefit from accepting a current proposal with the benefit to be obtained by rejecting the current proposal and waiting for future marriage proposals.

The analysis of this chapter can be extended in a number of directions. In what follows, we suggest two possible extensions. First, as discussed in the last paragraph of section 3.3, it would be useful to empirically determine what effect an increase in the rate at which marriage proposals are received has on the length of a marrying agent's waiting period. This will involve the specification and estimation of an appropriate econometric model.

Second, in order to capture the idea that marriage proposals are more likely to be received in certain time intervals in a marrying agent's lifetime, one can let the rate at which marriage proposals are received by the agent's well-wishers be a function of time. This will involve the analysis of a non-homogeneous Poisson process with an intensity function, say, $\beta(t)$, $t \geq 0$ A study of these aspects of the problem will permit richer analyses of the connections between the facilitative activities of well-wishers and the marrying agent's decision problem.

REFERENCES

Applbaum, K.D. "Marriage with the Proper Stranger: Arranged Marriage in Metropolitan Japan." *Ethnology* 34 (1995): 37-51.

Ahuvia, A.C., and M. Adelman. "Formal Intermediaries in the Marriage Market: A Typology and Review." *Journal of Marriage and the Family* 54 (1992): 452-63.

Atal, Y. (ed.). *The Changing Family in Asia*. UNESCO, Bangkok, Thailand, 1992.

Auboyer, J. *Daily Life in Ancient India*. New York: Macmillan Press, 1965.

Batabyal, A.A. "Aspects of Arranged Marriages and the Theory of Markov Decision Processes." *Theory and Decision* 45 (1998): 241-53.

———. "A Dynamic and Stochastic Analysis of Decision Making in Arranged Marriages." *Applied Economics Letters* 6 (1999): 439-42.

Becker, G.S. "A Theory of Marriage: Part I." *Journal of Political Economy* 81 (1973): 813-46.

———. *A Treatise on the Family*, enlarged ed. Cambridge: Harvard University Press, 1991.

Blood, R.O. *Love Match and Arranged Marriage: A Tokyo-Detroit Comparison*. New York: Free Press, 1967.

Chowdhury, A. "Family in Bangladesh." In *The Changing Family in Asia*, edited by Y. Atal. Bangkok, Thailand: UNESCO, 1992.

Croll, E. *The Politics of Marriage in Contemporary China.* Cambridge, U.K.: University Press, 1981.

Dixit, A.K., and Pindyck, R.S. *Investment Under Uncertainty.* Princeton, N.J.: Princeton University Press, 1994.

Goode, W.J. *World Revolution and Family Patterns.* New York: Free Press, 1963.

Harris, M. *Dynamic Economic Analysis.* New York: Oxford University Press, 1987.

Lavely, W. "Marriage and Mobility Under Rural Collectivism." In *Marriage and Inequality in Chinese Society,* edited by R.S. Watson and P.B. Ebrey. Berkeley, Cal.: University of California Press, 1991.

Mace, D., and Mace, V. *Marriage: East and West.* Garden City, N.Y.: Doubleday and Company, 1960.

Malhotra, A. "Gender and the Timing of Marriage: Rural-Urban Differences in Java." *Journal of Marriage and the Family* 59 (1997): 434-50.

Mandelbaum, D.G. *Society in India.* Berkeley: University of California Press, 1970.

Moore, M. "Changing India, Wedded to Tradition: Arranged Marriages Persist With 90s Twists." *Washington Post,* 8 October 1994.

Mullatti, L. "Changing Profile of the Indian Family." In *The Changing Family in Asia,* edited by Y. Atal. Bangkok, Thailand: UNESCO, 1992.

Otani, K. "Distributions in the Process to Marriage and Pregnancy in Japan." *Population Studies* 45 (1991): 473-87.

Pindyck, R.S. "Irreversibility, Uncertainty, and Investment." *Journal of Economic Literature* 29 (1991): 1110-52.

Rao, V.V.P., and Rao, V.N. *Marriage, the Family and Women in India.* New Delhi, India: South Asia Books, 1982.

Ross, S.M. *Introduction to Stochastic Dynamic Programming.* San Diego, Cal.: Academic Press, 1983.

———. *Stochastic Processes,* 2nd ed. San Diego, Cal.: Academic Press, 1996.

———. *Introduction to Probability Models,* 6th ed. San Diego, Cal.: Academic Press, 1997.

Turnbull, C.M., ed. *Africa and Change.* New York: Knopf, 1973.

Vatuk, S. *Kinship and Urbanization: White Collar Migrants in North India.* Berkeley: University of California Press, 1972.

Wolf, M. *Women and the Family in Rural Taiwan.* Stanford, Cal.: Stanford University Press, 1972.

NOTES

1. See Goode (1963), Mandelbaum (1970), Rao and Rao (1982), Otani (1991), and Moore (1994) for a more detailed corroboration of this claim.
2. For more on this literature, see Blood (1967), Wolf (1972), Turnbull (1973), Croll (1981), Lavely (1991), Atal (1992), Malhotra (1997), and the references cited in the previous endnote.
3. The meaning of "right" is made precise in Section 3. Further, in what follows, we shall conduct the analysis from the perspective of a male marrying agent; the analysis is

identical for a female agent.

4. In the context of western societies, Becker (1991, p. 324) too has referred to the salience of imperfect information in decision making in the marriage market.

5. For a more detailed description of the marriage related activities of well-wishers, see Mace and Mace (1960), Blood (1967), Vatuk (1972), and Ahuvia and Adelman (1992).

6. For more on the theory of optimal stopping, see Ross (1983), Harris (1987), and Dixit and Pindyck (1994).

7. The Poisson process is nicely discussed in Ross (1996, pp. 59-97) and in Ross (1997, pp. 249-302).

8. Batabyal (1999) has shown that the use of this kind of strategy is optimal in some circumstances.

9. The second order sufficient condition for a maximum is satisfied.

10. Note that if $T < (1/\beta)$ in equation (6.3), then $w^* = 0$. In this case, it is optimal to say yes to the very first marriage proposal that is received.

11. For more on this literature, see Pindyck (1991) and Dixit and Pindyck (1994).

12. The word "effective" here refers to the fact that the Child Marriage Act of 1930 provides penalties for the formalization of marriage for males under 18 and females under 14. See Chowdhury (1992) for additional details.

CHAPTER 7—
MEETINGS AND EXPOSURE BEFORE
AN ARRANGED MARRIAGE:
A PROBABILISTIC ANALYSIS

ABSTRACT

It is now common for parents and relatives of an individual seeking to have an arranged marriage to set up one or more meetings between this individual and the prospective spouses. As a result of these meetings, prospective spouses get exposed to this marrying individual. Even though this exposure level has a significant bearing on the eventual likelihood of marriage, as best as we can tell, the economics literature has paid no attention to the probabilistic attributes of meetings and the resultant level of exposure. As such, this chapter has three objectives. First, we analyze a simple stochastic model that focuses on the links between the trinity of meetings, exposure levels, and an arranged marriage. Next, we derive the conditional density function of the exposure level random variable under two assumptions about the eventual likelihood of marriage. Finally, we comment on an interesting property of a specific ratio of densities that is related to the above mentioned trinity.

Key words: arranged marriage, exposure, meetings, uncertainty

1. INTRODUCTION

Proponents of arranged marriages have always maintained that the presence of informational asymmetries and the proclivity of young people to seek physical pleasure together mean that young people generally cannot be relied upon to find a suitable spouse for themselves.[1] Consequently, parents, relatives, friends, and matchmaking intermediaries (hereafter facilitators) take upon themselves the task of looking for an appropriate bride or groom. Whereas in western nations, the individual wishing to marry typically looks for a spouse for himself or herself; in an arranged marriage this essential task is generally not undertaken by the individual but by his or her facilitators.[2] This is, in fact, a key difference between arranged marriages and marriages in western nations.

The second relevant characteristic of arranged marriages concerns the marrying individual's decision. As Rao and Rao (1982, pp. 32-33), Applbaum (1995), and Batabyal (2003) have pointed out, in modern arranged marriage settings, the individual wishing to marry has considerable autonomy over the actual marriage decision. In the words of Blood (1967, p. 11), while facilitators look for acceptable marriage candidates, the individual is "given an explicit opportunity to veto the nominee before negotiations are pursued." This opportunity to veto arises precisely because in contemporary arranged marriage settings, it is common for the marrying individual's facilitators to set up one or more meetings with prospective spouses. As a result of these meetings, prospective spouses get exposed to our marrying individual. Now, two things should be clear to the reader. First, this exposure level is a *random* variable. Second, this random variable has a significant bearing on the eventual likelihood of marriage.[3]

Given the discussion in the previous paragraph, it is interesting to ask what we currently know about the stochastic properties of the exposure level random variable. In this regard, recently, Batabyal (1998, 2001, 2003) has analyzed probabilistic models of decision making in arranged marriages. By using the so-called one stage look ahead policy, Batabyal (1998) demonstrates that a marrying individual's optimal decision rule depends only on the nature of the current marriage proposal, independent of whether there is a recall of previous proposals. In Batabyal (2001), decision making in arranged marriages with an overt age constraint is analyzed. In this setting, Batabyal (2001) shows that it is optimal to wait awhile before saying yes to a marriage proposal. What happens when a marrying individual decides to get married as long as the quality of a marriage proposal exceeds a stochastic reservation quality level? Batabyal (2003) provides an interesting answer to this question. First, he shows that the probability of getting married with this decision rule is always positive. Even so, he points out that, on average, an individual who uses this decision rule will end up single. This review of the small theoretical literature on arranged marriages in economics tells us that this literature has paid no attention to the stochastic properties of the exposure level random variable that we have discussed in the previous paragraph.

Given this state of affairs, we have three objectives in this chapter. First, in section 2.1 we analyze a simple stochastic model that focuses on the links between the trinity of meetings, exposure levels, and an arranged marriage. Second, in section 2.2 we derive the conditional probability density function of the exposure level random variable under two assumptions about the eventual likelihood of marriage. Third, in section 2.3 we comment on an interesting property of a specific ratio of densities that is related to the above-mentioned trinity. Finally, in section 3 we conclude and then we offer suggestions for future research on the subject of this chapter.

2. THE THEORETICAL FRAMEWORK

2.1. Preliminaries

Consider an individual who wishes to get married in an arranged marriage. As a result of the exploratory activities of this individual's facilitators, marriage proposals are brought to him.[4] If our marrying individual expresses interest in a particular proposal, then his facilitators will typically arrange one or more meetings with the woman behind the proposal. As a result of these meetings, two things happen. First, a potential spouse gets exposed to our marrying individual. Second, our marrying individual forms an opinion about a potential spouse, and, as a result, the meetings may increase or decrease the eventual likelihood of marriage with a particular woman.

Let us measure the exposure level of a potential spouse to our marrying individual with the random variable z. In our arranged marriage context, it is reasonable to suppose that an exposed potential spouse will eventually get wedded to our marrying individual with some probability. Let $Prob(z)$ denote this probability. Further, we suppose that the exposure level of a randomly selected member of the population of potential spouses has a probability density function given by $g(z)$.

Now two questions of interest arise. Our marrying individual's facilitators are interested in the exposure level random variable z, because the probability of marriage is a function of z. Put differently, these facilitators are interested in the stochastic properties of z conditional on a marriage being consummated. This is the first of our two questions.

In contrast, the interests of the people acting on behalf of potential spouses are somewhat different. Clearly, these people are also interested in the first question. However, because arranged marriages are common in more traditional societies in which pre-marital male/female associations are frowned upon, these people are risk-averse, and, hence, they will not want to diminish a woman's future marriage-ability by getting her too exposed—by way of meetings—to a man with whom eventual marriage is unlikely. From a mathematical standpoint, the upshot of all this is that people acting on behalf of the potential spouses are also interested in the stochastic properties of the exposure level random variable z but conditional on a marriage *not* being consummated. This is the second of our two questions. We now turn to a formal discussion of these two questions.

2.2. Two Density Functions

There are many ways to model the above two questions formally. However, it seems to us that the most reasonable way is to compute the conditional probability density function of the exposure level random variable z, first conditioned on a marriage taking place and then conditioned on a marriage not taking place. Mathematically speaking, we are interested in determining $g(z/marriage)$ and $g(z/no\ marriage)$.

Now, to compute $g(z/marriage)$, note that

$$g(z\,/\,marriage) = \frac{Prob\{marriage\,/\,z\}\,g(z)}{\int_{\forall z} Prob\{marriage\,/\,z\}\,g(z)\,dz}. \tag{7.1}$$

To simplify the expression on the right-hand-side (RHS) of equation (7.1), we shall use the fact that *Prob{marriage/z}* is given by *Prob(z)*. By using this piece of information, we can tell that

$$g(z \mid marriage) = \frac{Prob(z)g(z)}{\int_{\forall z} Prob(z)g(z)dz}. \tag{7.2}$$

Equation (7.2) gives us the answer to the first question that we posed in section 2.1. In particular, this equation tells us that the probability density function of the exposure level random variable z, conditional on a marriage being consummated, is given by the ratio of the product of the probability function *Prob(z)* and the density function $g(z)$ to the integral of the product of this probability and the density, the integration taking place over all relevant values of z.

We now turn to the second question of section 2.1. To compute the conditional probability density function *g(z/no marriage)*, we use the logic employed above to determine the answer to our first question. This gives us

$$g(z \mid no\ marriage) = \frac{\{1 - Prob(z)\}g(z)}{\int_{\forall z} \{1 - Prob(z)\}g(z)dz}. \tag{7.3}$$

We now have the answer to our second question in equation (7.3). Specifically, this equation tells us that the probability density function of the exposure level random variable z, conditional on no marriage taking place, is given by the ratio of the product of the complementary probability $\{1 - Prob(z)\}$ and the density function $g(z)$ to the integral of the product of this complementary probability and the density, the integration once again taking place over all relevant values of z.

What is the *optimal* level of exposure for potential spouses? This question is of considerable interest to both the marrying individual's facilitators and to the people acting on behalf of the potential spouses. In this connection, the conditional probability density functions in equations (7.2) and (7.3) are useful precisely because they can be used by our marrying individual's facilitators and by the people acting on behalf of the potential spouses to set up the objective function part of an appropriately formulated optimization problem. The solution to such a problem will yield an answer to the question posed at the beginning of this paragraph. We now comment on an interesting property of a specific ratio of densities that is related to the meetings/exposure level/arranged marriage trinity that we have been studying in this chapter.

2.3. A Ratio of Densities

Consider the ratio of the two densities given in equations (7.2) and (7.3). In other words, this ratio *g(z/marriage)/g(z/no marriage)* is the relative conditional probability density function of the exposure level random variable z. The question that we now wish to explore is the following: Is there a monotonicity relationship between the probability $Prob(z)$ and the ratio $g(z/marriage)/g(z/no\ marriage)$? In other words, is it the case that if $Prob(z)$ is increasing (decreasing) in z, then the above ratio is also increasing (decreasing) in z?

To answer this question, let us begin by writing down the mathematical expression for the ratio $g(z/marriage)/g(z/no\ marriage)$. Dividing the RHS of equation (7.2) by the RHS of equation (7.3), we get

$$\frac{g(z/marriage)}{g(z/no\ marriage)} = \left[\frac{\int_{\forall z} \{1 - Prob(z)\}g(z)dz}{\int_{\forall z} Prob(z)g(z)dz} \right] \frac{Prob(z)}{1 - Prob(z)}. \tag{7.4}$$

Now note that the expression in the square brackets on the RHS of equation (7.4) is ultimately *not* a function of z. Therefore, this expression will not affect our answer to the possible existence of a monotonicity relationship between the probability $Prob(z)$ and the ratio $g(z/marriage)/g(z/no\ marriage)$. As such, let us denote this expression inside the square brackets by C. By using this notation, we have

$$\frac{g(z/marriage)}{g(z/no\ marriage)} = C\frac{Prob(z)}{1-Prob(z)}. \tag{7.5}$$

Written in this way, equation (7.5) has a straightforward meaning. This equation tells us that the relative conditional probability density function of the exposure level random variable z can, for all practical purposes, be expressed as the ratio of the probability of getting married to the probability of staying single. Now, differentiating the RHS of equation (7.5) with respect to z we get

$$\frac{\{1-Prob(z)\}\,C\,Prob'(z)-C\,Prob(z)\{-Prob'(z)\}}{\{1-Prob(z)\}^2}, \tag{7.6}$$

where $Prob'(z)$ is the derivative of the probability with respect to z. Now, by inspecting the expression in (7.6) it is straightforward to verify that when $Prob'(z) > 0$, this expression is also positive. Similarly, when $Prob'(z) < 0$, this expression is also negative. We now conclude this section with two statements. First, we have just seen that a monotonicity relationship *exists* between the probability $Prob(z)$ and the relative conditional probability density function of the exposure level random variable z. Second, a study of the trinity of meetings, exposure levels, and an arranged marriage can, in this sense, be reduced to a study of this monotonicity relationship.

3. CONCLUSIONS

In this chapter we conducted a probabilistic analysis of the links between the trinity of meetings, exposure levels, and an arranged marriage. In particular, we first derived the conditional probability density function of the exposure level random variable z under two assumptions about the eventual likelihood of marriage. We then pointed out an interesting monotonicity relationship between the probability of marriage $Prob(z)$ and the relative conditional probability density function of the exposure level random variable z.

The analysis in this chapter can be extended in a number of different directions. In what follows, we suggest two possible extensions. First, as indicated in section 2.2, it would be useful to determine the optimal exposure level for the potential spouses by using the results in equations (7.2) and (7.3) to set up objective functions that can be used to formulate optimization problems for either our marrying individual's facilitators or for the people acting on behalf of the potential spouses. Second, it would also be helpful to further develop the stochastic setting of this chapter so that interaction effects can be examined between the facilitators of our marrying individual and the people acting on behalf of the potential spouses. Studies that analyze these aspects of the problem will enhance our understanding of the intricacies between meetings, exposure levels, and arranged marriages.

REFERENCES

Ahuvia, A.C., and M. Adelman. "Formal Intermediaries in the Marriage Market: A Typology and Review." *Journal of Marriage and the Family* 54 (1992): 452-63.

Applbaum, K.D. "Marriage with the Proper Stranger: Arranged Marriage in Metropolitan Japan." *Ethnology* 34 (1995): 37-51.

Auboyer, J. *Daily Life in Ancient India*. New York: Macmillan Press, 1965.

Batabyal, A.A. "Aspects of Arranged Marriages and the Theory of Markov Decision Processes." *Theory and Decision* 45 (1998): 241-53.

———. "A Dynamic and Stochastic Analysis of Decision Making in Arranged Marriages." *Applied Economics Letters* 6 (1999): 439-42.

———. "On the Likelihood of Finding the Right Partner in an Arranged Marriage." *Journal of Socio-Economics* 30 (2001): 273-80.

———. "On Decision Making in Arranged Marriages with a Stochastic Reservation Quality Level." *Applied Mathematics Letters* 16 (2003): 933-37.

Blood, R.O. *Love Match and Arranged Marriage: A Tokyo-Detroit Comparison*. New York: Free Press, 1967.

Goode, W.J. *World Revolution and Family Patterns*. New York: Free Press, 1963.

Mace, D., and V. Mace. *Marriage: East and West*. Garden City, N.Y.: Doubleday and Company, 1960.

Otani, K. "Time Distributions in the Process to Marriage and Pregnancy in Japan." *Population Studies* 45 (1991): 473-87.

Rao, V.V.P., and V.N. Rao. *Marriage, the Family and Women in India*. New Delhi, India: South Asia Books, 1982.

Vatuk, K. *Kinship and Urbanization: White Collar Migrants in North India*. Berkeley, Cal.: University of California Press, 1972.

NOTES

1. For more on these matters, see Goode (1963, p. 210), and Auboyer (1965, p. 176).
2. For a more detailed account of the activities of facilitators, see Mace and Mace (1960), Blood (1967), Vatuk (1972), Otani (1991), Ahuvia and Adelman (1992), and Batabyal (1999).
3. For additional details on these matters, go to http:www.askasia.org/frclasrm/ readings/rooo153.htm and to http://www.youthinformation.com/infopage.asp?snID=805 .
4. In the rest of this chapter, we assume that our marrying individual is a man. Obviously, this means that the proposals are from a variety of women or from people acting on behalf of women. The reader should note that our analysis goes through even if the marrying individual is a woman, but the salience of the second question that we ask later in this section declines if the marrying individual is a woman.

CHAPTER 8—
ARRANGED OR LOVE MARRIAGE?
THAT IS THE QUESTION

with Hamid Beladi

ABSTRACT

Although arranged and love marriages have been around for a long time, to the best of our knowledge, there are no *comparative* analyses in the economics literature of the relative merits of one or the other kind of marriage. As such, the purpose of this chapter is to conduct a theoretical inquiry into the desirability of arranged versus love marriages. We analyze a simple model of decision making in a dynamic and stochastic setting and show that the decision to have an arranged or a love marriage depends on a comparison of the expected amount of time it takes the agent's well-wishers to find a spouse with the expected total time it takes this agent to find a spouse by himself or herself.

Key words: arranged marriage, love marriage, optimal decision rule, dynamics, uncertainty

1. INTRODUCTION

Rudyard Kipling once said "Oh, East is East and West is West, and never the twain shall meet . . . ." Until recently, the same could be said about eastern-style arranged marriages and western-style love marriages. However, with the increasing mobility of people across the world, former easterners have become westerners and former westerners have, to a lesser extent, become easterners. This and related phenomena, such as a general rise in the education of women in the east, have resulted in a breakdown of the traditional barriers between eastern-style arranged marriages and western-style love marriages. In particular, many marrying agents now face a clear choice. They can either have an arranged marriage in which the agent's well-wishers[1] find a spouse for this agent, or they can try a love marriage in which the agent takes upon himself or herself the responsibility of finding a spouse.[2]

Scholars in disciplines other than economics have shown considerable interest in analyzing marriages in general and arranged marriages in particular.[3] However, with few exceptions, this interest has not been shared by economists in general. In fact, economists have been interested in systematically analyzing marriages only since Becker (1973). Further, this interest has largely been restricted to the study of western-style love marriages and related issues, in a deterministic setting. The fact that decision making processes in western-style love marriages are different from those used in eastern-style arranged marriages is not in contention. However, beyond recognizing this simple fact, economists have contributed very little to our understanding of the arranged versus love marriage choice that confronts many marrying agents today.

Given this state of affairs, this chapter has two objectives. First, we formulate a simple dynamic and stochastic model of marital decision making that explicitly focuses on the choice between an arranged and a love marriage. The reader should note that the purpose of this model is to shed light on the *hitherto unstudied* choice issue. As such, our modeling strategy will be deliberately parsimonious. We have intentionally avoided adding features to the model that would make the model more "realistic" but would also make the choice issue opaque. Second, we solve a simple optimization problem faced by a marrying agent and show that the decision to have an arranged or a love marriage depends on a comparison of the expected amount of time it takes the agent's well-wishers to find a spouse with the expected total time it takes this agent to find a spouse by himself.

The rest of this chapter is organized as follows: Section 2 provides an overview of decision making in arranged marriages and a review of the pertinent literature. Section 3 studies a dynamic and stochastic model of marital decision making and then discusses the factors that are germane in the arranged versus love marriage choice. Section 4 concludes and offers suggestions for future research.

2. AN OVERVIEW OF ARRANGED MARRIAGES AND THE EXTANT LITERATURE

Arranged marriages are predicated on the assumption that because of a number of reasons, such as the presence of imperfect and incomplete information (Goode, 1963, p. 210), and the tendency of young people to seek pleasure (Auboyer, 1965, p. 176), young persons generally cannot be relied upon to find a satisfactory spouse for themselves.[4] Therefore, a marrying agent's well-wishers take upon themselves the task of looking for a suitable bride. While in western-style love marriages, the agent wishing to marry generally looks for a spouse himself, in an arranged marriage, this salient task is generally *not* undertaken by the agent but by his well-wishers.[5] The reader should note that this is a fundamental difference between arranged and love marriages.

In recent times, economists have begun to explore a number of issues pertaining to western-style love marriages. For instance, Hu (2001) studied the ways in which the welfare system keeps families together. Nakosteen and Zimmer (2001) investigated the economic bases behind the spouse selection decisions of marrying agents. Finally, viewing children as irreversible investments, Fraser (2001) analyzed the nexuses between the number of children in marriage and higher income risk.

A small literature has addressed a few questions concerning eastern-style arranged marriages. Martin and Tsuya (1991) analyzed the effect that arranged marriages have on multi-generational co-residents in Japan. In their study of the sexual behavior of young couples in China, Feng and Quanhe (1996) analyzed the effects of moving away from traditional arranged marriages on the age at first marriage and on the length of the interval between marriage and the first birth. Batabyal (1998, 1999) has analyzed stochastic models of decision making in arranged marriages. Batabyal (1998) has shown that a marrying agent's optimal policy depends only on the nature of the current marriage proposal, independent of whether there is recall of previous proposals. In Batabyal (1999), it is shown that the marrying agent's optimal policy involves waiting a while, and saying yes to the first marriage proposal thereafter.

These papers have certainly advanced our understanding of various aspects of arranged and love marriages. Nevertheless, because there are *no* comparative analyses of the desirability of arranged versus love marriages, we still know very little about the factors that determine whether a marrying agent will seek an arranged or a love marriage. Batabyal (1998) has shown that a marrying agent's optimal policy depends only on the nature of the current marriage proposal, independent of whether there is recall of previous proposals. In Batabyal (1999) it is shown that the marrying agent's optimal policy involves waiting awhile, and then saying yes to the first marriage proposal thereafter. Given this state of affairs, we now use the theory of Poisson processes[6] to construct a theoretical model that will shed light on the choice of an arranged versus a love marriage.

3. THE THEORETICAL FRAMEWORK

3.1. Preliminaries

Consider an agent who has decided that he would like to get married. This agent now faces a choice. If he chooses the western-style love marriage route, then he takes upon himself the task of finding his wife. Alternately, he can select the eastern-style arranged marriage route. In this case, this agent's well-wishers find him his wife.

Suppose that our marrying agent chooses the love marriage route. In this case, he meets women in accordance with a Poisson process with rate β. If our agent decides to date a particular woman, then it takes the agent L units of time to decide whether he would like to marry this particular woman. If the agent decides that he would like to marry the woman in question, then he proposes to her, she accepts, and they are married right away. The reader will note that by saying "she accepts," we are bypassing the question of what happens when the woman in question rejects our marrying agent's proposal. If we permit this possibility, then the underlying model becomes significantly more complicated. Consequently, as noted at the end of section 1 and in the interest of analytical tractability, we disallow this possibility. The reader may want to think of the described sequence of events as one in which our agent meets women through a dating/marriage counseling service. In this case, all the women our agent meets wish to get married. As such, it makes more sense to suppose that a woman will not reject a marriage proposal.

For a variety of reasons, such as high search costs, our marrying agent may decide that he is better off with an arranged marriage. If our agent selects this route to marriage, then his well-wishers take upon themselves the task of finding him his wife. We model this aspect of the problem by supposing that the agent's well-wishers take a random amount of time to find a suitable wife. Denote the expectation of this time by A. In other words, on average, it takes the well-wishers A units of time to find our agent an apposite wife.

In order to accomplish his goal of getting married, our agent must follow some decision rule. A simple decision rule with a desirable property is the following.[7] Once the decision to get married has been made, our agent gives himself w units of time to be successful with the love marriage option. If he fails to find someone suitable by himself within w time units, then he gives the arranged marriage option a chance. The reader will note that the default option in this decision rule is love marriage. This aspect of the decision rule is consistent with reality (see Moore (1994) and Batabyal (2001)). Our first task now is to compute the expected time to marriage when our agent adopts the above decision rule.

3.2. Expected Time to Marriage

Because our marrying agent meets women in accordance with a Poisson process with rate β, the time until a woman arrives to meet our agent is exponentially distributed. As such, we can compute the expected time to marriage by conditioning on the time that a woman arrives to meet our agent. Using equation 1.5.1 in Ross (1996, p. 21), we get

$$E[\text{marriage time}] = \int_0^\infty E[\text{marriage time} / \text{woman arrives at } x]\beta \exp(-\beta x)dx , \quad (8.1)$$

where $E[\bullet]$ is the expectation operator. Now let us simplify the right-hand-side (RHS) of equation (8.1). This gives

$$E[\text{marriage time}] = \int_0^w (x + L)\beta \exp(-\beta x)dx + (w + A)\exp(-\beta w) . \quad (8.2)$$

We see that the expected time to marriage is the sum of two terms. The first term on the RHS of equation (8.2) is that portion of the expected time that arises from the pursuit of the love marriage option and the second term on the RHS of equation (8.2) is that portion of the expected time that originates from the pursuit of the arranged marriage option. This completes our computation of the expected time to marriage. We are now in a position to answer the central question of this chapter, i.e., the arranged or love marriage question.

3.3. Arranged or Love Marriage

Recall that our agent has already decided that he would like to get married. Consequently, one reasonable objective for him would be to choose w to minimize the expected time to marriage. In other words, our marrying agent solves

$$\min_{\{w\}} \left[\int_0^w (x+L)\beta \exp(-\beta x)dx + (w+A)\exp(-\beta w) \right]. \tag{8.3}$$

This is a straightforward but tedious minimization problem. By integrating the first term in the minimand and then by simplifying the resulting expression, we can restate the above minimization problem as

$$\min_{\{w\}} \left[\exp(-\beta w)\{A - L - (1/\beta)\} + (1/\beta) + L \right]. \tag{8.4}$$

Now by differentiating this minimand with respect to w yields

$$\frac{d\{E[marriage\ time]\}}{dw} = \exp(-\beta w)\{1 + \beta(L - A)\}. \tag{8.5}$$

Let us now interpret this equation carefully. Inspection of equation (8.5) tells us that when $\{(1/\beta) + L\} > A$, the above derivative is positive and hence the expected time to marriage is minimized by setting $w = 0$. Recall that because our marrying agent meets women in accordance with a Poisson process with rate β, the time until a woman arrives is exponentially distributed with mean $1/\beta$. Further, L is the time it takes our agent to decide whether he would like to propose to the woman he's dating. As such, $\{(1/\beta) + L\}$ is the expected total time it takes our agent to get married if he chooses the love marriage option. On the other hand, A is the expected amount of time it takes our agent's well-wishers to find him a wife. Consequently, the inequality $\{(1/\beta) + L\} > A$ tells us that if the expected total time taken to get married via the love marriage option exceeds the expected time it takes to get married via the arranged marriage option, then our agent should abandon the love marriage option (set $w = 0$) and instead choose the arranged marriage option.

On the other hand, when $\{(1/\beta) + L\} < A$, the expected total time to marriage via the love marriage option is less than the expected total time it takes to get married via the arranged marriage option. Consequently, in this case, our agent should forsake the arranged marriage option (set $w = \infty$) and instead go with the love marriage option. Finally, in the knife-edge case in which $\{(1/\beta) + L\} = A$, all values of w give the same expected time to marriage and hence our agent is indifferent between the arranged and the love marriage options.

The reader should note an interesting feature of our model. Specifically, while minimizing the expected time to marriage, we only considered the cases $w = 0$ and $w = \infty$. Indeed, in the model that we have just analyzed, we do *not* have to consider any other cases. This is because the time until a woman arrives to meet our marrying agent is exponentially distributed. Consequently, by the memoryless property of the exponential distribution,[8] it follows that if it is optimal to wait any time at all, then it is optimal to wait as long as it takes to get married.

4. Conclusions

In this paper we constructed a simple model to shed light on the *hitherto unstudied* question of the desirability of arranged versus love marriages. In particular, we analyzed the decision making process of a marrying agent who operates in a dynamic and stochastic environment. Our analysis shows that the choice between arranged and love marriages essentially reduces to a comparison of the expected total time it takes to find a wife in the love marriage option with the expected total time it takes to find a wife in the arranged marriage option. Put differently, this choice issue boils down to a comparison of our agent's own efficacy with the efficacy of his well-wishers.

The analysis contained in this chapter is novel but straightforward and hence it is possible to extend this analysis. In what follows, we suggest two possible extensions. First, in order to capture the idea that meetings with members of the opposite sex are more likely in certain time intervals in a marrying agent's lifetime, one can let the rate at which meetings occur be a function of time. This will involve the analysis of a non-homogeneous Poisson process with an intensity function, say, $\beta(t)$, $t \geq 0$.

Second, in section 3.1 we assumed that the recipient of a marriage proposal plays a passive role. This is a restrictive assumption. As such, it would be useful to conduct an analysis of the issues of this chapter in a game framework in which this recipient is able to respond strategically to a marriage proposal. A study of these aspects of the problem will permit richer analyses of issues relating to the desirability of arranged versus love marriages.

References

Ahuvia, A.C., and Adelman, M. "Formal Intermediaries in the Marriage Market: A Typology and Review." *Journal of Marriage and the Family* 54 (1992): 452-63.

Atal, Y., ed. *The Changing Family in Asia.* Bangkok, Thailand: UNESCO, 1992.

Auboyer, J. *Daily Life in Ancient India.* New York: Macmillan Press, 1965.

Batabyal, A.A. "Aspects of Arranged Marriages and the Theory of Markov Decision Processes." *Theory and Decision* 45 (1998): 241-53.

———. "A Dynamic and Stochastic Analysis of Decision Making in Arranged Marriages." *Applied Economics Letters* 6 (1999): 439-442.

————. "On the Likelihood of Finding the Right Partner in an Arranged Marriage." *Journal of Socio-Economics* 30 (2001): 273-280.

Becker, G.S. "A Theory of Marriage: Part I." *Journal of Political Economy* 81 (1973): 813-46.

————. *A Treatise on the Family*, enlarged edition. Cambridge, Mass.: Harvard University Press, 1991.

Blood, R.O. *Love Match and Arranged Marriage: A Tokyo-Detroit Comparison.* New York: Free Press, 1967.

Croll, E. *The Politics of Marriage in Contemporary China.* Cambridge, U.K.: Cambridge University Press, 1981.

Feng, W., and Y. Quanhe. "Age at Marriage and the First Birth Interval: The Emerging Change in Sexual Behavior Among Young Couples in China." *Population and Development Review* 22 (1996): 299-320.

Fraser, C.D. "Income Risk, the Tax-Benefit System, and the Demand for Children" *Economica* 68 (2001): 105-25.

Goode, W.J. *World Revolution and Family Patterns.* New York: Free Press, 1963.

Hu, W. "Welfare and Family Stability: Do Benefits Affect When Children Leave the Nest?" *Journal of Human Resources* 36 (2001): 274-303.

Kulkarni, V.G. *Modeling and Analysis of Stochastic Systems.* London, U.K.: Chapman and Hall, 1995.

Lavely, W. "Marriage and Mobility Under Rural Collectivism." In *Marriage and Inequality in Chinese Society*, edited by R.S. Watson and P.B. Ebrey. Berkeley: University of California Press, 1991.

Mace, D., and V. Mace. *Marriage: East and West.* Garden City, N.Y.: Doubleday and Company, 1960.

Malhotra, A. "Gender and the Timing of Marriage: Rural-Urban Differences in Java." *Journal of Marriage and the Family* 59 (1997): 434-50.

Mandelbaum, D.G. *Society in India.* Berkeley: University of California Press, 1970.

Martin, L.G., and N.O. Tsuya. "Interactions of Middle-Aged Japanese With Their Parents." *Population Studies* 45 (1991): 299-311.

Moore, M. "Changing India, Wedded to Tradition: Arranged Marriages Persist With 90s Twists." *Washington Post*, 8 October 1994.

Nakosteen, R.A., and M.A. Zimmer. "Spouse Selection and Earnings: Evidence of Marital Sorting." *Economic Inquiry* 39 (2001): 201-13.

Rao, V.V.P., and V.N. Rao. *Marriage, the Family and Women in India.* New Delhi, India: South Asia Books, 1982.

Ross, S.M. *Stochastic Processes*, 2nd ed. San Diego, Cal.: Academic Press, 1996.

Turnbull, C.M. (ed.) *Africa and Change.* New York: Knopf, 1973.

Vatuk, S. *Kinship and Urbanization: White Collar Migrants in North India.* Berkeley: University of California Press, 1972.

Wolf, M. *Women and the Family in Rural Taiwan.* Stanford, Cal.: Stanford University Press, 1972.

NOTES

1. By well-wishers, we mean parents, relatives, friends, and matchmaking intermediaries.
2. In what follows, we shall conduct the analysis from the perspective of a male marrying agent. However, the reader should note that the analysis is identical from the perspective of a female agent.
3. For more on this, see Goode (1963), Blood (1967), Mandelbaum (1970), Wolf (1972, Turnbull (1973), Croll (1981), Rao and Rao (1982), Lavely (1991), Atal (1992), Moore (1994), and Malhotra (1997).
4. Becker (1991, p. 324), too, referred to the significance of imperfect information in decision making in western-style love marriages.
5. For a more detailed account of the marriage-related activities of well-wishers, see Mace and Mace (1960), Blood (1967), Vatuk (1972), and Ahuvia and Adelman (1992).
6. For lucid accounts of the Poisson process, see Kulkarni (1995, pp. 186-238) and Ross (1996, pp. 59-97).
7. Batabyal (1999, 2001) showed that the use of this kind of decision rule is optimal in some circumstances.
8. For additional details on this property, see Kulkarni (1995, pp. 189-190) and Ross (1996, pp. 35-38).

CHAPTER 9—
ON STRATEGY AND THE
LIKELIHOOD OF SUCCESS IN
MARITAL MATCHMAKING
UNDER UNCERTAINTY

ABSTRACT

In contemporary times, in both the East and in the West, individuals wishing to get married have made increasing use of matchmakers. This notwithstanding, economists have paid scant attention to the strategies employed by matchmakers and to the likelihood of success arising from the use of these strategies. Consequently, this chapter has two objectives. First, we specify a "local" and then a "global" strategy for matching male and female clients and then we compute the expected total cost to a matchmaker from the use of these strategies. Next, we calculate the mean number of successes that our matchmaker can hope for. Finally, we provide an upper bound on the probability that the number of matching successes is at least $1 + \theta$ times the mean number, where θ is any positive number.

Key words: matchmaking, marriage, strategy, success, uncertainty

1. INTRODUCTION

Arranged marriages have traditionally been more popular in the East than in the West. As pointed out by Blood (1967), Moore (1994), Batabyal (2001), and Batabyal and Beladi (2002), in arranged marriages, it is common to use matchmakers.[1] Matchmakers typically meet friends, family members, and increasingly the individuals wishing to get married, and they then attempt to pair male and female candidates with similar aspirations, goals, and interests. Clearly, the matchmaker's objective is to ensure that the paired individuals do in fact get married and that this marriage lasts for an appreciable amount of time. It is important to note that matchmaking activities are fundamentally prospective; further, all matchmakers operate in inherently stochastic environments.

Until recently, most marrying individuals in the West took upon themselves the task of finding a suitable mate. Consequently, matchmaking activities in general were rather limited. However, in the past two decades, owing to a variety of reasons not the least of which is a general lack of time, this state of affairs has changed substantially. As a result, today, even in the West, it is quite common to find a plethora of matchmakers advertising their services in newspapers and on the internet.[2] Given the traditional use of matchmakers in the East and the increasing popularity of matchmakers in the West, a number of interesting questions about the activities of these matchmakers emerge. Examples of such questions include the following. What are the properties of alternate matchmaking strategies? Given a particular matching strategy, what is the expected number of successes that a matchmaker can hope for? Finally, given a desired number of successes, is it possible to make a mathematically precise statement about the probability that the number of matching successes will be at least the desired number? Although these questions are both thought-provoking and relevant, unfortunately, economists have paid virtually no attention to them.

Quah (1990) has discussed the phenomenon of matchmaking but the basic focus of his paper is on analyzing the factors influencing the age at first marriage. More recently, Van Raalte and Webers (1998) have studied a two-sided market in which one type of agent needs the services of a matchmaker in order to be matched to the other type. In this setting, these authors analyze a scenario in which match-makers compete for agents of both types by means of commission fees. Finally, in a model of two-sided search, Bloch and Ryder (2000) have shown that when a matchmaker charges a uniform participation fee, only agents of higher quality participate in the centralized matching procedure. In contrast, if the matchmaker charges a commission on the matching surplus, then only agents of lower quality go to this intermediary. Although these papers have certainly advanced our understanding of issues related to matchmaking, nonetheless, the questions mentioned in the previous paragraph remain unanswered.

Consequently, our chapter has two objectives. First, we specify two desirable strategies—the "local" strategy and the "global" strategy—for matching male and female clients and then we compute the expected total cost to a matchmaker from the use of each of these strategies.[3] Next, we calculate the expected number of matching successes that a matchmaker can hope for and then we provide an upper bound on the probability that the number of matching successes is at least $1 + \theta$ times the mean number, where θ is any positive number. The rest of this chapter is organized as follows. Section 2 describes the theoretical framework and the two matchmaking strategies that comprise the subject of this chapter. Section 3 computes the average total cost to a matchmaker from the use of each of these strategies. Section 4 calculates the mean number of matching successes and then it shows how the upper bound discussed above can be derived. Section 5 concludes and discusses avenues for further research on the subject of this chapter.

2. THE THEORETICAL FRAMEWORK

Consider a matchmaker who has a number of male and female clients who wish to get married. Specifically, there are n male and n female clients and our match-maker's job is to match each male client to one and only one female client. Now, the task of matching male and female clients involves the expenditure of some—and possibly considerable—effort on the part of the matchmaker. Put differently, every time the matchmaker assigns a male client to a female client, he incurs a cost.

To this end, let $c(j, k)$ be the cost incurred by our matchmaker when he matches male client j to female client k, $j, k = 1, \ldots, n$.

Clearly, there are many possible strategies that our matchmaker could use to carry out the task of assigning each male client to one female client. However, to fix ideas, we shall consider the following two desirable strategies in this chapter. The first or "local" matching strategy works as follows. The matchmaker begins by assigning male client 1 to the female client which results in the lowest cost to him. In other words, male client 1 is matched with female client k_1, where $c(1, k_1) = \min_{\{k\}} c(1,k)$. Female client k_1 is then removed from further consideration. Then the matchmaker assigns male client 2 to female client k_2 so that $c(2, k_2) = \min_{\{k \neq k_1\}} c(2,k)$. The matchmaker continues in this manner until all male and female clients have been matched. This local strategy is desirable because it always selects the best female match for the male client currently under consideration.

Our matchmaker's second desirable strategy is a "global" version of the previous paragraph's local strategy. Using this global strategy, the matchmaker first considers all n^2 cost values and he selects the pair (j_1, k_1) for which his cost $c(j, k)$ is minimal. The matchmaker then matches male client j_1 to female client k_1. Next, he eliminates from further consideration all cost values that involve either male client j_1 or female client k_1. As a result, $(n - 1)^2$ cost values now remain and our matchmaker continues the process of selecting pairs and then matching as just described. Put differently, at every stage, he chooses the male and the female clients that result in the lowest cost among all the unmatched male and female clients. We have already explained why the previous paragraph's local strategy is desirable. Simply put, this global strategy is desirable because it is a more thorough version of the local strategy. Our task now is to compute the average total cost incurred by our matchmaker when he uses each of these two strategies.

3. THE LOCAL AND THE GLOBAL EXPECTED TOTAL COSTS

As indicated in section 1, our matchmaker operates in a stochastic environment. To model this aspect of the problem, we let all the cost values $c(j, k)$ comprise a set of independent random variables. Now, when analyzing greedy type algorithms, it is common to work with exponential random variables.[4] Consequently, in the remainder of this section, we suppose that the n^2 cost values $c(j, k)$ constitute a set of independent, exponentially distributed, random variables with rate β.

3.1. The Local Expected Total Cost

Given that our matchmaker is using the local strategy, let $c(j, \bullet)$ denote the cost associated with matching male client j, $j = 1, \ldots, n$. It should be clear to the reader that $c(1, \bullet)$ is the minimum of n independent exponential random variables, each of which has rate β. Hence, using equation 5.6 in Ross (2000, p. 249), it follows that $c(1, \bullet)$ is itself exponentially distributed with rate βn. Similarly, $c(2, \bullet)$ is the minimum of n - 1 independent exponential random variables with rate β and, hence, $c(2, \bullet)$ is exponentially distributed with rate $\beta(n - 1)$. Continuing in this manner we can tell that $c(j, \bullet)$ is exponentially distributed with rate $\beta(n - j + 1), j = 1, \ldots, n$.

Using the above information, we conclude that the expected total cost to the matchmaker when he uses the local strategy, $E_l[total\ cost]$, is

$$E_l[total\ cost] = E[c(1, \bullet) + \ldots + c(j, \bullet) + \ldots + c(n, \bullet)] = E_l(c(1, \bullet) + \ldots +$$
$$E_l[c(j, \bullet)] + \ldots + E_l[c(n, \bullet)]. \tag{9.1}$$

Now, using the properties of the exponential distribution, the n expectations on the right-hand-side (RHS) of equation (9.1) can be simplified. This simplification yields

$$E_l[total\ cost] = \frac{1}{\beta n} + \ldots + \frac{1}{\beta(n-j+1)} + \ldots + \frac{1}{\beta} = \frac{1}{\beta}\left[\sum_{j=1}^{j=n}\frac{1}{j}\right]. \tag{9.2}$$

The RHS of equation (9.2) gives us the expected total cost to our matchmaker when he uses the local strategy to match his male and female clients. We see that this cost is the product of the mean of the exponentially distributed cost values and a summation term. We now compute our matchmaker's average total cost when he uses the global strategy.

3.2. The Global Expected Total Cost

Let $c(j, \bullet)$ be the cost of the jth male-female pair matched by this global strategy. Because $c(1, \bullet)$ is the minimum of all the n^2 $c(j, k)$ cost values, by using equation 5.6 in Ross (2000, p. 249) we can tell that $c(1, \bullet)$ is exponentially distributed with rate βn^2. Now, because exponentially distributed random variables have the memoryless property,[5] we reason that the amounts by which the other $c(j, k)$ exceed $c(1, \bullet)$ will be independent and exponentially distributed random variables with rates β. Hence, $c(2, \bullet)$ equals the sum of $c(1, \bullet)$ and the minimum of $(n - 1)^2$ independent exponentials with rate β. Similarly, $c(3, \bullet)$ is equal to the sum of $c(2, \bullet)$ and the minimum of $(n - 2)^2$ independent exponentials with rate β, and so on.

Now, by using the above reasoning and the properties of exponentially distributed random variables, we infer that $E[c(1, \cdot)] = 1/(\beta n^2)$, $E[c(2, \cdot)] = E[c(1, \cdot)] + 1/\{\beta(n-1)^2\}$, and $E[c(3, \cdot)] = E[c(2, \cdot)] + 1/\{\beta(n-2)^2\}$. Continuing this line of reasoning, we get $E[c(k, \cdot)] = E[c(k-1, \cdot)] + 1/\{\beta(n-k+1)^2\}$ and finally $E[c(n, \cdot)] = E[c(n-1, \cdot)] + 1/\beta$. These expressions for the various cost expectations can be simplified even further. This simplification yields $E[c(1, \cdot)] = 1/(\beta n^2)$, $E[c(2, \cdot)] = 1/(\beta n^2) + 1/\{\beta(n-1)^2\}$, and eventually $E[c(n, \cdot)] = 1/(\beta n^2) + 1/\{\beta(n-1)^2\} + \ldots + 1/\beta$.

By using the above computations, we conclude that the expected total cost to our matchmaker when he uses the global strategy, $E_g[total\ cost]$, is

$$E_g[total\ cost] = \frac{n}{\beta n^2} + \frac{(n-1)}{\beta(n-1)^2} + \frac{(n-2)}{\beta(n-2)^2} + ... + \frac{1}{\beta}. \qquad (9.3)$$

Further simplifying the RHS of equation (9.3), we get

$$E_g[total\ cost] = \frac{1}{\beta}[\frac{1}{n} + \frac{1}{n-1} + \frac{1}{n-2} + ... + 1] = \frac{1}{\beta}[\sum_{j=1}^{j=n} \frac{1}{j}]. \qquad (9.4)$$

Inspecting equations (9.2) and (9.4), it is clear that we have just established

Theorem 1: *The expected total cost to our matchmaker is the same for both strategies.*

Theorem 1 contains a rather surprising result. Specifically, this theorem tells us that it does not matter which strategy our matchmaker uses because both strategies lead to the same total expected cost. Intuitively, one expects greater thoroughness on the part of the matchmaker to increase his costs. However, in the setting of this chapter, this is not the case. Having said this, the reader should note that greater painstakingness does not, however, result in a lower expected total cost. Consequently, from the standpoint of the expected total cost criterion, our matchmaker will be indifferent between the local and the global strategies.

What is the expected number of successes that our matchmaker can hope for from either strategy? Moreover, given a desired number of successes, is it possible to say something mathematically precise about the probability that the number of matching successes is at least the desired number? We now address these two questions.

4. SUCCESS IN MATCHING: TWO QUESTIONS

Before we proceed any further with the above two questions we must first delineate the meaning of a success. Recall that the whole point of matchmaking is to ensure that marriages eventually take place. Consequently, in what follows, we shall say that a match is a success if it leads to marriage within T time periods. The actual value of T will typically vary from society to society and, *ceteris paribus*, we expect T to be shorter in eastern societies than in western societies. This notwithstanding, it is clear that there has to be a temporal dimension to the meaning of success. Moreover, it is also clear that for it to be interesting, an analysis of the "expected number of matching successes" question must be conducted from an *ex ante* perspective and not T time periods after the n male-female pairings have been made.

4.1. The Expected Number of Successes

Suppose that our matchmaker observes the n matches that he has just made. Also suppose that our matchmaker's skill is such that the probability that each match is a success (will lead to marriage in T time periods) is $p \in (0, 1)$. What is the expected number of successes? To answer this question, it is useful to think of the n matches as n independent Bernoulli random variables.[6] Now let $S(n)$ denote the number of successes from n matches. Then, by using the properties of Bernoulli random variables, we see that

$$E[S(n)] = np. \tag{9.5}$$

In other words, the average number of successes is given by the product of the number of matches and the success probability of each match. Inspecting equation (9.5), it is clear that holding the number of matches fixed, the expected number of successes is an increasing function of the success probability p. Similarly, keeping the success probability p fixed, as we increase the number of matches, the expected number of successful matches rises. Let us now address the question about the probability that the number of matching successes is at least some desired number.

4.2. Computing the Upper Bound

From section 4.1 we know that the expected number of matching successes is np. Now given this expected number, suppose that our matchmaker desires a certain number of successes. We would like to make a mathematically precise statement about the probability that the actual number of successes is at least the desired number times the expected number of successes np.

To address this question, let us begin by letting $\theta > 0$ be any positive number. Further, suppose that our matchmaker's desired number of successes is $1 + \theta$ times the expected number of successes. We will now provide an upper bound[7] on the probability that the desired number of successes is $1 + \theta$ times the expected number of successes. By using corollary 3.1.2 in Ross (2002, p. 77), we see that

$$Prob\ \{S(n) - E[S(n)] \geq \theta E[S(n)]\} \leq \exp\{-2(\theta E[S(n)])^2 / n\}. \tag{9.6}$$

Because $E[S(n)] = np$, the RHS of inequality (9.6) can be simplified. This gives

$$Prob\ \{S(n) - E[S(n)] \geq \theta E[S(n)]\} \leq \exp\{-2(n(p\theta)^2\}. \tag{9.7}$$

In other words, the probability that the number of matching successes is at least $1 + \theta$ times the expected number of successes np is bounded above by the exponential term on the RHS of inequality (9.7). In particular, this probability is at most as large as the reciprocal of the exponential raised to $2n(p\theta)^2$. By inspecting inequality (9.7), we see that holding the number of matches n and the success probability p fixed, the probability of interest decreases to zero exponentially fast as θ increases. This tells us that if we use the expected number of successes np as our benchmark, then there is a tradeoff between a higher desired number of matching successes and the probability that these desired successes will in fact materialize.

5. CONCLUSIONS

In this paper we analyzed three hitherto unstudied questions about the nature of decision making in marital matchmaking. First, we established the counterintuitive result (see Theorem 1) that the local and the global strategies both lead to the same expected total cost to our matchmaker. Second, we showed that the expected number of successes that our matchmaker can hope for is given by the product of the number of matches n and the success probability p. Finally, we pointed out that given a desired number of matching successes, it is possible to provide an upper bound on the probability that the actual number of successes is at least this desired number.

The analysis in this chapter can be extended in a number of directions. In what follows, we suggest two possible extensions. First, in section 3, we studied the expected total cost to our matchmaker resulting from the use of local and global strategies. Although these strategies are desirable in the sense indicated in section 3, it would nonetheless be useful to determine the set of matches that minimizes the sum of the n costs that are incurred.

Second, it would also be useful to study the matchmaking function within the context of a model of common agency. In such a model, the matchmaker would be the common agent serving two principals, namely, a representative male client and a representative female client. An analysis of these aspects of the problem will allow richer analyses of the nexuses between alternate pairing strategies and the outcome of matchmaking in stochastic environments.

REFERENCES

Batabyal, A.A. "On the Likelihood of Finding the Right Partner in an Arranged Marriage." *Journal of Socio-Economics* 30 (2001): 273-80.

Batabyal, A.A., and H. Beladi. "Arranged or Love Marriage? That is the Question." *Applied Economics Letters* 9 (2002): 893-97.

Bloch, F., and H. Ryder. "Two-Sided Search, Marriages, and Matchmakers." *International Economic Review* 41 (2000): 93-115.

Blood, R.O. *Love Match and Arranged Marriage: A Tokyo-Detroit Comparison.*

New York: Free Press, 1967.

Moore, M. "Changing India, Wedded to Tradition: Arranged Marriages Persist with 90s Twists." *Washington Post*, 8 October 1994.

Quah, E. "Optimal Search, Matchmaking and the Factors Affecting Age at First Marriage." *Indian Economic Journal* 37 (1990): 74-80.

Ross, S.M. *Introduction to Probability Models*, 7th ed. San Diego, Cal.: Harcourt Academic Press, 2000.

———. *Probability Models for Computer Science*. San Diego, Cal.: Harcourt Academic Press, 2002.

Van Raalte, C., and H. Webers. "Spatial Competition with Intermediated Matching." *Journal of Economic Behavior and Organization* 34 (1998): 477-88.

Winston, W. *Operations Research Applications and Algorithms*. Cambridge, Mass.: Duxbury Press, 1997.

NOTES

1. In the rest of this chapter, we suppose that our matchmaker is a single male individual. Even so, we recognize that the matchmaker may be a single female individual or even a firm. In this regard, the point to note is that except for minor stylistic changes, nothing in our analysis is altered by accounting for these last two possibilities.

2. See the "Personals" section of the *New York Times*, the *Boston Globe*, and internet sites such as www.Udate.com and www.match.com .

3. These strategies are variants of the so-called "greedy algorithms." For more on these algorithms and related issues such as the assignment problem, see Winston (1997) and Ross (2000, 2002).

4. See Ross (2000, p. 250; 2002, p. 36) for additional details on this point.

5. For more on this, see Ross (2000, pp. 243-45; 2002, p. 33).

6. See Ross (2000, pp. 27-28; 2002, pp. 6-7) for more on Bernoulli random variables.

7. This bound is also called the Chernoff bound. See Ross (2002, pp. 76-78) for additional details.

CHAPTER 10—
A GAME MODEL OF DOWRY
DETERMINATION IN AN ARRANGED
MARRIAGE CONTEXT

ABSTRACT

In many arranged marriage contexts, a mediator assists the bride and the groom's families in determining the actual amount of the dowry. Although social scientists in general and economists in particular have studied many aspects of dowries, to the best of our knowledge, the nature of the interaction between a mediator and the two concerned parties has not been analyzed previously in the literature. Therefore, the purpose of this chapter is to analyze a simple game model of dowry determination. Specifically, we first solve for the Nash equilibrium pair of final dowry offers from the two concerned parties. Next, we show how the equilibrium dowry offers optimally trade off the desire to make an assertive offer with the likelihood that this offer will be selected by the mediator.

Key words: arranged marriage, dowry, game model, mediator, uncertainty

1. INTRODUCTION

The word "dowry" refers to a practice in Hindu society in which payments in cash and/or kind are made by the family of the bride to the family of the groom at the time of marriage. Because most marriages in Hindu society in a country like India are arranged, the practice of dowry has a fundamental connection with the custom of arranging marriages for one's children.[1] Sheel (1999) has noted that the origins of the phenomenon of dowry can be traced back to Vedic times in which expensive clothes, jewelry, and other items were frequently given voluntarily to both the bride and to the groom's families during the so-called *kanyadan* or "giving the daughter away" ceremony. As such, the original purpose of dowry was to sanctify material wealth and also to augment one's status at the time of marriage.

In contemporary times however, the practice of dowry has changed substantially. In a disproportionate number of arranged marriages in India and elsewhere, dowry payments are anything but voluntary. In addition, Leslie (1998) and others have pointed out that such payments are now often used by the groom's family to impoverish the bride's family by extracting large amounts of cash and/or material resources as a precondition for marriage. The groom's family is able to do this because women tend to occupy an inferior position in India's patrilineal kinship and family system.

The actual amount of the dowry that is demanded in any particular instance is closely related to the economic and to the social status of the groom's family. In this regard, Sheel (1999, p. 18) tells us that the higher the socioeconomic status of the groom's family, the higher is generally the demand for dowry. This state of affairs naturally gives rise to two questions: First, how do the concerned parties come to an agreement over the actual amount of the dowry payment? Second, if a mediator is used, what is the nature of the interaction between this mediator and the bride and the groom's families?

Extant research by social scientists in general and economists in particular provides a clear answer to the first question and this answer is twofold.[2] We learn that in some arranged marriage settings, the bride and the groom's families directly negotiate with each other to determine the amount of the dowry. However, Jaggi (2001) and Reddy (2002) have clearly noted that in many other arranged marriage settings, the two concerned parties conduct the negotiations with the help of a *mediator*. This leads us to the second question of the previous paragraph. Although there now exists a large literature in the social sciences on dowries and economists themselves have contributed to increasing our understanding of alternate aspects of dowries,[3] to the best of our knowledge, there is no research—either by economists or by other social scientists—on the nature of the interaction between a mediator and the bride and the groom's families.

Given this state of affairs, the purpose of this chapter is to construct and analyze a simple game-theoretic model of dowry determination in which the interests of the two concerned parties and those of the mediator are explicitly accounted for. Specifically, in section 2.1, we describe our game theoretic model of the dowry determination problem. Section 2.2 sets up and then solves the bride and the groom's optimization problems. Section 2.3 uses an example to illustrate the working of our model. Section 3 concludes and offers suggestions for future research on the subject of this chapter.

2. THE GAME THEORETIC MODEL

2.1. Preliminaries

It should be clear to the reader that, in general, there are a variety of ways in which a mediator can interact with the bride's family and the groom's family to determine the amount of the dowry payment. Therefore, rather than model all the different kinds of mediation, for concreteness, in the rest of this chapter we shall think of the mediator as an arbitrator. Our game model of dowry determination is based on Farber (1980) and the game itself is a static game of complete information.[4] There are three players. First, there is a representative from the bride's family who we shall refer to as the *bride b*. Second, there is a representative from the groom's family who we shall refer to as the *groom g*. Finally, there is a mediator who we shall designate with the letter *m*.

The timing of the game between the bride, the groom, and the mediator is as follows. First, the bride and the groom simultaneously make dowry offers d_b and d_g, respectively. Second, the mediator selects one of the above two offers as the final dowry amount that is agreed upon by both the bride and the groom. Because the mediator generally has some knowledge of both the bride and the groom, we suppose that this individual has a preferred dowry amount in mind. Let us denote this preferred amount by d_m. Further, to keep the mathematics from getting unduly complicated, we suppose that after observing the offers d_b and d_g, the mediator simply picks the offer that is closer to his preferred amount d_m.

Clearly, from everything we know about actual dowries, we expect the offer made by the bride to be less than that made by the groom. Mathematically, we expect $d_g > d_b$ in equilibrium and in our subsequent analysis we shall show that this is indeed the case. Given that the above inequality holds in equilibrium, the mediator's choice problem can be described as follows. He chooses d_b if $d_m < (d_b + d_g)/2$ and he chooses d_g if $d_m > (d_b + d_g)/2$.

The mediator obviously knows d_m but neither the bride nor the groom knows the mediator's preferred dowry amount. In other words, from the standpoint of the bride and the groom, d_m is a *random* variable. As such, we suppose that the bride and the groom both believe that the cumulative distribution function of d_m is $H(d_m)$ and that its density function is $h(d_m)$. With this stochastic specification and given our delineation of the mediator's choice problem in the previous paragraph, we can deduce that

$$Prob\{d_b \text{ is selected}\} = Prob\{dm < \frac{d_b+d_g}{2}\} = H(\frac{d_b+d_g}{2}), \qquad (10.1)$$

and

$$Prob\{d_g \text{ is selected}\} = 1 - H(\frac{d_b+d_g}{2}). \qquad (10.2)$$

Now, by combining equations (10.1) and (10.2), we can tell that the mediator's expected dowry amount is $d_b \cdot Prob\{d_b \text{ is selected}\} + d_g \cdot Prob\{d_g \text{ is selected}\}$. In turn, this expectation can be written as

$$d_b \bullet H(\frac{d_b+d_g}{2}) + d_g \bullet [1 - H(\frac{d_b+d_g}{2})] . \qquad (10.3)$$

In general, the bride will want the dowry to be as low as possible and, in contrast, the groom will want the dowry to be as high as possible. Therefore, we suppose that the bride wants to *minimize* the mediator's expected dowry amount (given by equation (10.3)) and that the groom wants to *maximize* this same amount.

2.2. The Optimization Problems

Formally, the bride solves

$$\min_{\{d_b\}} [d_b \bullet H(\frac{d_b+d_g}{2}) + d_g \bullet [1 - H(\frac{d_b+d_g}{2})]] \ , \qquad (10.4)$$

and the groom solves

$$\max_{\{d_g\}} [d_b \bullet H(\frac{d_b+d_g}{2}) + d_g \bullet [1 - H(\frac{d_b+d_g}{2})]] \ . \qquad (10.5)$$

Now, using the result that $H'(\cdot)=h(\cdot)$, the first-order necessary conditions for an optimum for the above two optimization problems are

$$H(\frac{d_b^*+d_g^*}{2}) = \frac{(d_g^*-d_b^*)}{2} \bullet h(\frac{d_b^*+d_g^*}{2}) \qquad (10.6)$$

and

$$1 - H(\frac{d_b^*+d_g^*}{2}) = \frac{(d_g^* - d_b^*)}{2} \bullet h(\frac{d_b^*+d_g^*}{2}). \qquad (10.7)$$

where d_b^* and d_g^* are the optimizing values of the two control variables in problems (10.4) and (10.5), respectively.

Inspecting equations (10.6) and (10.7) we see that the RHSs of these two equations are equal. Therefore, setting the LHSs of these two equations equal, we get

$$H(\frac{d_b^*+d_g^*}{2}) = \frac{1}{2}. \qquad (10.8)$$

In other words, equation (10.8) tells us that in equilibrium, the *mean* of the two dowry offers from the bride and the groom must equal the *median* of the mediator's preferred dowry amount. Now substituting the result from equation (10.8) into either equation (10.6) or equation (10.7), we get

$$[h(\frac{d_b^*+d_g^*}{2})]^{-1} = d_g^* - d_b^*. \qquad (10.9)$$

Equation (10.9) tells us that the gap between the two dowry offers made by the groom and the bride (the RHS) must equal the reciprocal of the value of the density function at the median of the mediator's preferred dowry amount (the LHS). Now, in order to proceed further with the analysis, it will be helpful to make an assumption about the distribution of our mediator's preferred dowry amount d_m. Therefore, we suppose that d_m is normally distributed with mean μ and variance σ^2. This supposition means that $h(d_m)=\{1/\sqrt{(2\pi\sigma^2)}\}\exp[-\{1/(2\sigma^2)\}(d_m-\mu)^2]$.

2.3. An Example

It is well-known that the normal distribution is symmetric about its mean and, hence, the mean μ equals the median for this distribution. In our case, this means that equations (10.8) and (10.9) can be rewritten as

$$\frac{d_b^*+d_g^*}{2} = \mu \quad and \quad d_g^* - d_b^* = \frac{1}{h(\mu)} = \sqrt{(2\pi\sigma^2)}. \tag{10.10}$$

Solving the two equations in (10.10) simultaneously gives us the bride and the groom's Nash equilibrium dowry offers. Mathematically, we have

$$d_b^* = \mu - \sqrt{(\frac{\pi\sigma^2}{2})} \quad and \quad d_g^* = \mu + \sqrt{(\frac{\pi\sigma^2}{2})}. \tag{10.11}$$

In other words, equation (10.11) tells us two things. First, the equilibrium dowry offers made by the bride and the groom are centered around the mean of the mediator's preferred dowry amount (μ). Second, the difference between these two offers is essentially a function of the bride and the groom's uncertainty about the mediator's preferred dowry amount (σ^2). Specifically, as σ^2 increases (decreases), this difference between the two equilibrium dowry offers also increases (decreases).

The equilibrium described by equations (10.10) and (10.11) makes perfect economic sense and it is also consistent with what we know to be true about real world dowries. To see this clearly, note that when presenting their dowry offers, the bride and the groom face a very basic tradeoff. A very low offer by the bride or a very high offer by the groom results in a better reward if this offer is selected by the mediator. However, a very low or a very high offer also makes it less likely that this offer will, in fact, be chosen by the mediator. Therefore, when there is a great deal of uncertainty about the mediator's preferred dowry amount, i.e., when σ^2 is high, the bride and the groom can afford to make more assertive offers because these more assertive offers are unlikely to be completely at odds with the mediator's preferred dowry amount. In contrast, when there is little or no uncertainty, i.e., when σ^2 is equal to or close to zero, neither the bride nor the groom can afford to make "very assertive" offers because the mediator is more likely to accept the dowry offer that is close to his preferred mean amount (μ).

We close this section by pointing out that the above kind of analysis—with the normal distribution—also can be conducted for other distribution functions. For instance, consider the case in which the mediator's preferred dowry amount d_m follows a beta distribution. In this case $h(d_m)=[\Gamma(\alpha+\beta)/\{\Gamma(\alpha)\Gamma(\beta)\}]d_m^{\alpha-1}(1-d_m)^{\beta-1}$,

$\alpha > 0$, $\beta > 0$, and $\Gamma(\cdot)$ is the gamma function. When the parameters α and β are equal to each other, $h(d_m)$ is symmetric about ½ the mean, and, hence, the mean equals the median. With some additional clutter, the analysis for this beta distribution case would proceed exactly as indicated earlier in this section.

3. CONCLUSIONS

In this chapter, we analyzed a simple game model of dowry determination. In particular, we first solved for the Nash equilibrium dowry offers from both the bride and the groom. Then, with the help of an example, we showed how the equilibrium dowry offers optimally trade off the desire—on the part of both the bride and the groom—to make an assertive offer with the likelihood that this assertive offer will, in fact, be selected by the mediator.

The analysis in this chapter can be extended in a number of directions and, in what follows, we suggest two potential extensions. First, it would be useful to extend the static game analysis of this chapter to a dynamic game analysis in which the three players do not interact once and for all but, instead, interact over several time periods. Second, it would be instructive to examine the case in which the bride and the groom have heterogeneous beliefs about how the mediator's preferred dowry amount (d_m) is distributed. Studies that analyze these aspects of the problem will increase our understanding of the properties of mediated dowry determination in arranged marriage contexts.

REFERENCES

Agnihotri, I. "The Expanding Dimensions of Dowry." *Indian Journal of Gender Studies* 10 (2003): 307-19.

Anderson, S. "Why Dowry Payments Declined with Modernization in Europe but are Rising in India." *Journal of Political Economy* 111 (2003): 269-310.

Batabyal, A.A. "Aspects of Arranged Marriages and the Theory of Markov Decision Processes." *Theory and Decision* 45 (1998): 241-53.

———. "Meetings and Exposure Before an Arranged Marriage: A Probabilistic Analysis." *Applied Economics Letters* 11 (2004): 473-76.

Batabyal, A.A., and H. Beladi. "Spouse Selection in Arranged Marriages: An Analysis of Time Invariant and Time Variant Decision Rules." *Journal of Economic Research* 8 (2003): 187-201.

Bloch, F., and V. Rao. "Terror as a Bargaining Instrument: A Case Study of Dowry Violence in Rural India." *American Economic Review* 92 (2002): 1029-43.

Bumiller, E. *May You be the Mother of a Hundred Sons.* New Delhi, India: Penguin, 1990.

Dalmia, S. "A Hedonic Analysis of Marriage Transactions in India: Estimating Determinants of Dowries and Demand for Groom Characteristics in Marriage." *Research in Economics* 58 (2004): 235-55.

Dalmia, S., and P.G. Lawrence. "The Institution of Dowry in India: Why it Continues to Prevail." *Journal of Developing Areas* 38 (2005): 71-93.

Farber, H.S. "An Analysis of Final-Offer Arbitration." *Journal of Conflict Resolution* 24 (1980): 683-705.

Fudenberg, D., and J. Tirole. *Game Theory*. Cambridge, Mass.: MIT Press, 1991.

Gibbons, R. *A Primer in Game Theory*. Hemel Hempstead, U.K.: Harvester Wheatsheaf, 1992.

Jaggi, T. "The Economics of Dowry: Causes and Effects of an Indian Tradition." *University Avenue Undergraduate Journal of Economics* 4 (2001): 1-19. <http://www.econ.ilstu.edu/UAUJE>

Leslie, J. "Dowry, Dowry Deaths, and Violence Against Women: A Journey of Discovery." In *South Asians and the Dowry Problem*, edited by W. Menski. London, U.K.: Trentham Books Limited, 1998.

Menski, W., ed. *South Asians and the Dowry Problem*. London, UK: Trentham Books Limited, 1998.

Rao, V. "The Rising Price of Husbands: A Hedonic Analysis of Dowry Increases in Rural India." *Journal of Political Economy* 101 (1993): 666-77.

Reddy, S. "Ancient Practice of Dowry Perpetuates Violence Against Women in India." *Digital Freedom Network*. http://www.asiaobserver.com/India-story2.htm> (2002).

Sharma, U. "Dowry in North India: Its Consequences for Women." In *Family, Kinship, and Marriage in India*, edited by P. Uberoi. New Delhi, India: Oxford University Press, 1993.

Sheel, R. *The Political Economy of Dowry*. New Delhi, India: Manohar Publishers, 1999.

NOTES

1. The reader should note that even though our discussion of dowry is in the context of arranged marriages in Hindu society in a country like India, the phenomenon of dowry is also prevalent in the context of arranged marriages in other religions and in other nations. For good general accounts of the phenomenon of dowry, the reader should consult Bumiller (1990), Menski (1998), and Sheel (1999). For more on decision making in arranged marriages, see Batabyal (1998, 2004) and Batabyal and Beladi (2003).

2. For a more detailed discussion of this point, see Sharma (1993), Rao (1993), Agnihotri (2003), and Dalmia (2004).

3. For more on research by economists on alternate aspects of dowries, see Rao (1993), Bloch and Rao (2002), Anderson (2003), Dalmia (2004), and Dalmia and Lawrence (2005).

4. For more on static games of complete information, see Fudenberg and Tirole (1991, Chapter 1), or Gibbons (1992, Chapter 1).

INDEX

ABOUT THE AUTHOR

Amitrajeet A. Batabyal is Arthur J. Gosnell Professor of Economics at the Rochester Institute of Technology, in Rochester, New York. He earned a B.S. in Agricultural Economics with Honors and Distinction at Cornell University in 1987, an M.S. in Agricultural and Applied Economics at the University of Minnesota in 1990, and a Ph.D. in Agricultural and Resource Economics at the University of California, Berkeley, in 1994. Professor Batabyal has taught undergraduate courses in international economics, benefit-cost analysis, and intermediate microeconomics, and graduate courses in environmental economics, microeconomic theory, and operations research.

Professor Batabyal has published over 350 books, book chapters, journal articles, and book reviews. He has received many awards and honors, including the Geoffrey J.D. Hewings Award from the North American Regional Science Council in 2003, the Moss Madden Memorial Medal from the British and Irish section of the Regional Science Association International in 2003, and the Outstanding Achievement in Research Award from the Society for Range Management in 2006. He is currently the Book Review Editor of the *American Journal of Agricultural Economics*, an Associate Editor of the *Journal of Regional Science*, an Editorial Council member of the *Review of Development Economics*, and an Editorial Board member of the *Asian-African Journal of Economics and Econometrics*. His research interests lie in environmental and natural resource economics, international trade theory, development economics, and the interface of economics with biology, philosophy, and political science. He is often interviewed by the regional and national media for his views on a variety of economic issues.